BAD PETS
Save Christmas!

ALLAN ZULLO

Scholastic Inc.

To my niece and nephew, Delaney and McKinley Benson, whose love and compassion toward others embody the true meaning of Christmas
— A.Z.

ISBN 978-0-545-61229-6

15 14 13 12   16 17 18/0

Printed in the U.S.A.   40
First Scholastic printing, November 2013

CONTENTS

AUTHOR'S NOTE

Do you ever get the feeling that sometimes we drive our pets a bit crazy during the holidays? We don't intend to confound them, but sometimes we do, all in the joyful spirit of Christmas. We fasten reindeer antlers to the dog's head. We dress the cat in an elf costume. We make Fido sit perfectly still for holiday pictures. We set out dishes of chocolates, candies, and treats and expect Sparky to resist temptation.

No wonder that by Christmas Day, our normally well-behaved pets sometimes get into trouble!

In this book, you'll read about outrageously naughty dogs and cats, a monkey, a horse, a pig, and a gang of raccoons that each turned the holidays into an unforgettable time. Each story is based on, or inspired by, true-life events and has been dramatized with recreated dialogue and scenes. The names and places have been changed.

These tales prove that no matter how badly our pets behave, they can still create wonderful holiday memories that last a lifetime.

MOJO'S YULETIDE MAGIC

The Merrick boys knew better than to complain while helping their mom, Katie, decorate the Christmas tree. True, the tree wasn't big or pretty — money was tight this year as always — but under her direction, the homely blue spruce was turning into a holiday showpiece.

Ryan, 13, and Colin, 11, didn't utter a peep of protest when they had to find the one faulty Christmas bulb that darkened a whole strand. Nor did they whine when Katie made them move ornaments from one branch to another for "better balance." They went along with the program because they saw how happy the decorating made her. Ever since her breakup two weeks earlier with the man everyone, including the widowed Katie, thought she would marry, she had been down in the dumps.

Katie stepped back and studied the tree with her trained eye as a department-store window-display designer. "We need some bigger ornaments to hide the gaps," she said.

Ryan sifted through the box of leftover decorations and pulled out a frayed cutout Christmas tree made of construction paper with a photo pasted on it. "What about this one? I made it when I was in fourth grade."

The photo showed Katie hugging her brother, a lanky man whose curly brown hair was topped by a green-and-white striped elf's hat. Holding a sprig of mistletoe above his head, the boys' uncle sported a pair of ruby-red wax lips below his thick brown mustache.

"Tell me again why he's called Uncle Skitch," Colin said to his mother.

"Ever since he was a kid, he was known as Skitch the Stitch because he could make anyone laugh," Katie replied. Then she sighed. "It's been three years now."

"I remember he was always cracking jokes," said Ryan. "Any idea where he is?"

Before she could answer, they heard dogs barking in the front yard, and the doorbell. Ryan answered the door and faced a man in his 30s clad in a bright red long-sleeve cycling jersey and matching long tights and gloves.

"Do you own that dog?" the cyclist demanded, squinting in anger as he pointed to the furiously barking rust-colored knee-high canine a few feet away.

"Yes, that's Mojo," answered Ryan after ordering the dog to hush and shoving him inside. "Is there a problem, sir?"

"That dog of yours caused me to crash!" the cyclist claimed. "I'm riding down the street when I look ahead and see your dog playing with two mutts in your yard. Suddenly, your dog leads a charge and starts racing toward me, barking like crazy. I speed up, thinking I can get past him before he reaches me, but he's fast and runs right out in front of me. I swerve and the next thing I know I'm kissing pavement."

The neighbor's dogs, a beagle and a mixed-breed spaniel, stood across the street, still barking at the cyclist.

"Your dog charged me for no reason," the man said.

"Well, sir, there actually is a reason. When he was a puppy, Mojo was hit by a bright red truck. He was transported to the animal hospital wrapped in a red blanket, and the nurses there were wearing red scrubs. He's hated red ever since."

The cyclist threw up his hands in exasperation. "That's the most absurd thing I've ever heard." He stomped off, shouting over his shoulder, "That dog is a menace! He needs to be confined!"

Luckily for Mojo, he lived in a county where dogs were free to roam. True to his breed, the Finnish spitz was a 35-pound bundle of energy whose intelligence and friendliness (except to those who wore red) were equaled only by his independence and stubbornness.

Nothing — other than a cage — could keep him confined without consequences. The Merricks learned early on that when he wanted to go out, they should let him out. The few times they ignored him, he busted through the screen door or slipped out an open window. One time he was poised to leap from a second-floor window before Ryan grabbed him. The deep claw marks in the back door were a testament to his resolve.

The fenced-in backyard couldn't contain him because he repeatedly dug his way to freedom. Katie refused to use a shock collar on him or chain him. No, the only way to keep him happy was to let him wander the rural neighborhood in the Colorado foothills, where most residents possessed a free-spirited attitude of "Don't tell me what to do, and I won't tell you what to do."

Everyone local knew Mojo . . . and he knew everyone. With a face resembling that of a red fox and a plumed bushy tail that curled over his hindquarters, he would prance down the street, looking for a kid or another dog to play with. If he knew you, he liked you. Anyone not from the neighborhood, such as the cyclist, could expect to experience a nonstop barrage of barking from Mojo, who loved the sound of his voice. The only way to shut him up was to give him a treat or bend down and offer to pet him, at which point he considered you a friend for life.

Mojo was the poster child for his breed (which is the national dog of Finland) — adventurous, good-natured, lively, and loyal. He was best known for gathering a canine posse. He often went house to house, barking until the neighbors let out his four-legged pals, such as Wags and Apollo (the dogs from across the street) and PeeWee, Merlin, Cleo, Taffy, and Blondie. Mojo was the Mr. Good Times of the canine world, leading a parade to the home of Mrs. Toolan, who fed them her homemade pumpkin balls, or to Old Man Rainey, who tossed them scraps from his latest hunting trips. It wasn't unusual to see Mojo at the head of the pack as they tried — almost always unsuccessfully — to corner chipmunks, squirrels, rabbits, and neighborhood cats. The dogs' owners weren't pleased with Mojo's ability to sniff out smelly things, such as dead fish, for his pals and him to roll around in. Lately, though, several owners had expressed concern that Mojo was taking the pack farther away than usual from their modest working-class neighborhood.

"You know how much we adore Mojo," Talia Denard, the owner of Taffy the cocker spaniel, told Katie two days after the incident with the cyclist. "But I'm worried his roaming is going to get him and other dogs in trouble. On my way home from work today, I spotted him and Taffy a few blocks from the underpass where those homeless people hang out. That's a half mile away."

"Oh, that's not good," said Katie.

"I'm keeping Taffy locked up in the house the next few days, because I don't want her following Mojo that far from home."

"I totally understand, Talia," said Katie. "I'll try to keep closer tabs on him."

That night at dinner, Katie told the boys that she wanted to curb Mojo's roaming.

"Good luck with that," said Colin. "Maybe we could tie five-gallon jugs of water to his collar to slow him down," he cracked.

Eventually, the conversation shifted to their church's Christmas food drive. "We've already topped last year's effort," Katie said. "Missy's Barbecue Shack donated two cases of baked beans."

"Didn't Uncle Skitch steal a case of baked beans, and that's why he left all of a sudden?" asked Colin.

Katie took a deep breath and shoved her plate aside. "You boys are old enough to learn the truth. When you were much younger, Skitch had everything going for him — a wife and baby daughter, a nice home, and a good job as the general manager of Masters Motors. But he loved booze more than his family and his work. After your aunt Karla divorced him and moved away, he got drunk, took the boss's car, and totaled it. Naturally, he lost his job. He couldn't find work and had no money and eventually lost the house. That's when he moved in with us at Christmas and promised to stay sober."

"He didn't stay very long," Ryan said.

"No, he didn't," said Katie. "I discovered he had taken out all the cans of baked beans from a case intended for the Christmas food drive and replaced them with his empty booze bottles. I threw him out of the house that very night, and, as you know, no one has seen or heard from him for the past three years. Frankly, I don't know if he's dead or alive."

"We knew something must have happened," said Ryan. "And then, you know, we hear things from relatives."

"Boys, I'm sorry I wasn't completely honest at the time. I wanted to spare you the details so you'd have good memories of your uncle Skitch."

"Do you miss him?" Ryan asked.

"Of course. He's my brother."

"Would you give him another chance?" asked Colin.

"Only if he was sober or truly wanted to get sober," she said.

The phone rang, and Ryan took the call. It was from Talia Denard, who lived two blocks away. "Would you please come and get Mojo?" she requested. "He wants Taffy to play, and I won't let her out. He's lying in the middle of the street and won't move."

"Have you thought of throwing a few snowballs at him?" Ryan asked.

"Please, come get your dog before he gets run over."

After playing rock-paper-scissors to see who would retrieve Mojo, the loser, Colin, found the dog sprawled in the quiet gravel street in front of the Denard house. Tire tracks from the season's first snow — a three-inch accumulation overnight — indicated that two cars had driven around the dog. When Colin called Mojo, the dog obediently got up and followed him home.

The next day, Mojo went out on his morning rounds. The sun was shining and the temperature was rising enough to melt most of the snow. Because it was the start of Christmas vacation, the boys were helping their mother collect donations for the food drive. When the family returned home early in the afternoon, Mojo was frolicking in the front yard with a smallish gray-and-white Siberian husky. None of the Merricks had seen the dog before. It had no collar.

As Katie and the boys stepped out of the car, Mojo walked over to them. The husky followed, wagging its tail. "She sure is friendly," said Colin, rubbing the dog's face. "I wonder who she belongs to."

The dogs played for the next half hour, until Mojo barked to be let inside. When Colin opened the door, the husky trailed Mojo into the house and made a beeline for the dog dish. She wolfed down all the dry food. With Katie's approval, Colin filled the dish again only to have the husky gobble that portion, too.

"That's one hungry dog," Colin said. "Do you think she's been abandoned?"

"She's a little skinny, but otherwise looks like she's been well cared for," Katie replied.

"I'm surprised that Mojo didn't protect his dog

dish," said Ryan. "He just sat there and watched her eat. He must have known she was hungry."

After filling her belly, the husky nuzzled Katie, played with the boys, and then napped with Mojo. At dusk, as it started to snow again, Katie scooted the husky outside. "Go home," she ordered. "Go home now, before the weather gets really nasty."

After dinner, Mojo paced back and forth, whimpering and scratching at the door. When Colin let him out, the boy noticed that the husky was still in the yard. "Hey, Mom, that dog never left. And it's snowing real hard."

"All right, let her in," Katie said. "We'll keep her for the night."

The two dogs lay next to each other by the floor vents in the living room and fell asleep. The next day — which was frigid, windy, and snowy — Katie didn't have the heart to kick out the sweet-tempered husky. "Tomorrow, on the way to the food bank, we'll take her to the animal shelter," she told the boys.

When they brought the husky to the shelter, the dog went over and licked the hand of a young staffer named Marlee.

"Has anyone reported missing a female Siberian husky?" Katie asked her.

"As a matter of fact, a homeless man came in here every day last week, asking if someone had brought in a husky," Marlee replied. "He told me that a thug had stolen his Siberian — he called her his daughter — while he slept under the freeway overpass north of here." Pointing to the husky, she said, "She definitely matches the description he gave me."

Marlee pulled out a scanner to determine if a microchip had been implanted in the husky. There was none.

"This could be his dog," said Marlee. "The man said he was sure the dog was kidnapped, because her leash wasn't attached to her collar and it was gone along with some dog treats and twenty dollars that he had hidden under his hat.

"It was heartbreaking. He told me, 'Now that she's gone, I don't know what to do. Dogs are everything when you are homeless. They keep you going and listen to you when you have no one to talk to.' He said he couldn't sleep without her, that she'd been his only companion since she was just a puppy. He said, 'I can't live without her. She was like my daughter.' He really loves that dog."

"When was the last time you saw him?" Katie asked.

"It's been a few days," said Marlee. "I hope he didn't give up or move on."

"Did he leave his name or say where we can find him?" Katie asked.

"All he gave me was a first name — Bob. No address, because he lives on the streets. Homeless shelters don't allow dogs. My guess is he could be anywhere within walking distance of the animal shelter. In this nasty weather, he's probably camping under a bridge or overpass. Then again, without his dog, maybe he's staying in a homeless shelter."

Colin gently squeezed Katie's arm and said, "Mom, let's go look for him."

"Well, I don't know . . ."

"Come on, Mom," urged Ryan. "Wouldn't it make a wonderful Christmas present if we could reunite the man with his dog?"

"Boys, you're right," she declared. "Let's do it!"

At the boys' insistence, Katie decided the family would keep the husky until the owner was found. She gave Marlee her name, address, and phone number and told her to call if Bob ever showed up again. Before they left, the staffer provided them with a description of the homeless man: late 40s; six feet tall; skinny; bushy brown beard and mustache; wearing a soiled olive-drab army field jacket, jeans, black stocking cap, and army boots.

With the husky in the car, the Merricks drove around to the places where drifters and vagabonds were known to camp. But because of the snowy conditions, there were few wanderers, and none fit Bob's description. Of those Katie questioned, no one recognized the dog.

When the family returned home, Mojo and the husky were delighted to see each other and playfully wrestled and chased each other. While the boys prepared LOST posters, Katie called several homeless shelters but had no success in finding Bob.

The next morning, she let the dogs out amid snow flurries. By the time the family was dressed and heading out the door to volunteer at the church's Christmas Eve lunch for the disadvantaged, the dogs had disappeared. "Boys, let's take a quick spin around the neighborhood and try to find those two," said Katie.

About five blocks away, they drove up behind Mojo and the husky, who were trotting along the side of the road. They weren't ambling or stopping to sniff some new scent. Their strides were purposeful, as if they had a destination in mind.

"We'll take them with us to the church hall," Katie said. "There'll be plenty of homeless there. Maybe someone will recognize her."

She pulled ahead of the dogs and then, with some effort, coaxed them into the car. As the vehicle neared a clump of pine trees by the freeway overpass, the husky suddenly became agitated and began barking in a high pitch and pawing at the window.

"She wants out," said Colin.

Katie stopped the car and Ryan opened the door. The husky bolted straight for the stand of trees, barking all the way. Mojo was running right behind her, followed by Ryan, Colin, and Katie.

As the husky disappeared in the trees, the Merricks heard a voice shout, "Stella! Stella! You came back!"

Reaching the trees, the trio spotted a bearded man in an army jacket on his knees, holding the happy husky, who was licking his face. "Oh, Stella, I've been so lost without you," he cried.

Caught up in the joyous reunion, Mojo hopped around them in a circle. The thick branches of the trees had shielded the ground from the snow. In front of a blue tarp that had been strung from one pine to another were the charred remains of an extinguished campfire. A tattered backpack lay nearby.

The man buried his head into the husky's side and wept. He was unaware of the Merricks until Katie spoke. "Are you Bob?"

Startled, the man looked up at the three of them, then pulled his black stocking cap down to his eyebrows and lowered his head. "Yeah, I'm Bob."

"Is that your dog?" she asked.

"Yeah. She's been gone for ten days," he said without looking up. "Someone stole her. She must have escaped from him, because her collar is missing."

"We've been taking care of her the last four days," Katie said. "Our dog, Mojo, brought her home. We've been trying to find the owner. We went to the animal shelter, and they told us about you. We've driven all over the area looking for you."

"Thank you for caring for her," he said, still keeping his face away from them. "She's all I have."

"Tell you what," said Katie. "We're heading over to help serve a Christmas Eve lunch at our church. Why don't you and Stella join us?"

"That's nice of you, but I'll pass. I'm fine here, now that Stella is with me."

Suddenly, Katie inhaled deeply, as if she had been struck with a revelation. She clasped her hands together and hesitated before speaking. "This is quite a coincidence," she said. "I have a brother named Bob, although no one called him that. And he has a daughter named Stella."

"I think you better go," he muttered, staring at the ground. "You don't want to be late for lunch."

"Before I leave, let me introduce myself. I'm Katie Merrick and these are my sons, Ryan and Colin."

Without looking at them, he gave a little wave. "Nice to meet you."

The boys started to walk away, but Katie motioned for them to stay. She bent down in front of Bob, gently lifted off his stocking cap, and cradled his scruffy face in her hands. "Hello, Skitch," she murmured, her eyes brimming with tears.

"Hello, Katie."

They threw their arms around each other and wept, their bodies heaving with every breath. The flabbergasted boys plopped to the ground in silence as the realization sunk in: Their long-lost uncle had been found!

When Katie and Skitch finally pulled themselves apart, he confessed, "I'm so ashamed. I was hoping you wouldn't recognize me."

"How could I not? You're my brother."

"I was afraid you'd never want anything to do with me ever again."

"Nonsense. You and Stella will come home with us."

Skitch closed his eyes and wiped his nose with the back of his hand. "Katie, oh, Katie, this is a Christmas dream come true."

"What happened to you, Skitch? Where have you been?"

"After you threw me out of the house — which I deserved — I stayed with some friends in Cheyenne, but then they sent me packing. Too much drinking. I couldn't find work because I've had back problems since the car accident. I had no money for rent, so I started living on the street. I was panhandling and going in and out of shelters and getting an occasional day-labor gig. I was still drinking a lot. Then I won Stella in a card game when she was a pup, and that changed everything.

"She captured my heart. She depended on me for everything, so I quit drinking cold turkey. The trouble was I just couldn't find any work. And I couldn't stay in any homeless shelters unless I gave up Stella. There was no way I was going to do that.

"So we've just been living hand to mouth, hitching rides through Wyoming, Nebraska, Kansas, and Colorado. I was just passing through here when I fell and wrenched my back. I was in so much pain that I couldn't move for a few days. Stella never left my side.

23

She comforted me and licked my face. Then one night, someone stole her and my money, what little I had. I was devastated. I nearly lost my mind. I checked the animal shelter every day until my back went out on me again and I couldn't walk, so I holed up here. I wanted to die. And then . . ." He started to weep. "And then Stella runs into my arms . . . and you and the boys appear. How is that even possible?"

"Some might call it fate," Katie said. "I call it Mojo."

LEAP OF FAITH

Audrey Rodenbach scooped up her cat, Midnight, held him in front of her, and twirled around. "We're going to spend Christmas with Auntie El in New York City!" she squealed. "Isn't that super amazing?"

As the ten-year-old girl spun on her heel, her long raven hair, which matched the color of her cat's fur, flew wildly in the air. Midnight batted at the closest strands before Audrey put him down on her bed. Being with her great-aunt was always fun, because Auntie El — that's what Audrey called her aunt Eleanor — treated her like a princess. Eleanor could afford to, because she had plenty of money, mostly from her divorce settlement with her multimillionaire ex-husband. For a girl from a small town in Indiana, like Audrey, going to the Big Apple during the holidays was the trip of a lifetime.

Audrey couldn't wait to see the tricked-out window displays along Fifth Avenue, the fabulous shows, the soaring Christmas tree at Rockefeller Center, and all the decorations that adorned the streets of Manhattan. The plan called for Audrey and her parents, Ida and Bill, who were both college professors, to fly to New York for the week and stay with Eleanor in her spacious three-bedroom Park Avenue apartment. The plan did not call for Midnight to accompany them — a situation that Audrey hoped to change.

About two weeks before the trip, Audrey brought up the subject with her parents at the breakfast table. "Please, please, please can we take Midnight to New York?" she begged.

"Sorry, pumpkin," Bill said. "He's not flying with us. Your cat is always getting into mischief, and your great-aunt wouldn't appreciate having a cat climb all over her nice, expensive furniture. He's better off here."

"But, Daddy, the last time we went on vacation and left him at the kennel, he went missing for two days."

Bill smiled. "I still don't know how he ended up in their supply room cabinet."

"A *tightly shut* cabinet," Ida reminded him.

"Well, that won't happen this time," Bill said. "He's staying at home. Mrs. Orosco will come over and feed him every day and change his litter box."

Crestfallen, Audrey shuffled off. As she passed the laundry room, she heard a strange clunking sound coming from the dryer. "Mom, I think there's something wrong with the dryer," she called out.

Ida went to the appliance, stopped it, and opened the lid. She peered inside and screamed. Then she reached in and pulled out Midnight, who was limp and extremely hot. His eyes were closed and his tongue was hanging out.

Audrey gasped and instinctively covered her mouth with her hands in shock. Tears streamed down her cheeks before she could utter, "Is . . . he . . . dead?"

"He's barely breathing," Ida replied. "Oh, this is awful!"

Bill rushed into the room. "Midnight was in the dryer?" he asked in disbelief.

"We have to save him!" Audrey cried out.

Bill took the drooping cat from Ida and ran out into the frosty December air. "Quick, help me gather some snow!" he shouted. About an inch of snow had fallen the day before. With their bare hands, the three of them scraped up what little snow remained and packed it around the distressed animal to cool him off.

Then they rushed him to the veterinarian. While they sat in the waiting room, Ida figured out what had happened to Midnight. "I put a load of clothes in the dryer last night, and I forgot to take them out when they were done," she explained. "When I opened the lid this morning, the clothes seemed a little wrinkled, so I decided to fluff them up. Midnight must have leaped into the dryer when I turned my back to get the fabric softener. I didn't notice him among the dark clothes when I closed the lid." Her voice cracked when she added, "I put the dryer on high."

"Is he going to die?" Audrey asked.

Bill squeezed her hand and replied, "Dr. Ling is a fine vet. She's doing everything she can to save him. They say cats have nine lives. Well, that cat of yours still has a few left."

"Not many," Ida said. "He spent the night in the trunk of my car last winter. . . ."

"And when he was a kitten, he got trapped in the sleeper sofa," added Audrey.

"Yes," said Bill. "Then there were the two days in that cabinet, and before that, there was the day we found him in the attic and had to rush him to the vet's for heat exhaustion."

An hour later, Dr. Ling entered the waiting room and announced, "Midnight will be okay. He was basically in shock. Considering that he was twirling around in a dryer heated to one hundred sixty degrees, I'd say it's pretty remarkable that he's alive. His ears are burned, and his tail is slightly injured. He also has some fluid in his lungs caused by exertion from constantly trying to right himself as the dryer spun. The bottom line is that he should make a full recovery."

Audrey bounded over to the vet and gave her a big hug. "Thank you! Thank you! Can we take him home now?"

"Let's keep him overnight, just to be safe," said Dr. Ling. "I think the only reason Midnight survived is that the clothes in the dryer were already dry. Had they been wet, the pounding from those soaked, heavy clothes would have killed him."

A few days after the dryer incident, Audrey made another pitch to her parents for bringing Midnight to New York. She tried working on their sympathies, hoping to convince them that because of the trauma the cat had endured, he needed to be with family. Her parents patiently listened and then rendered their verdict: "The cat stays home."

On the morning of their flight, Midnight was lounging on the chest of drawers in Audrey's room as Ida helped her daughter pack. The excitement of going to New York had eased some of the heartache Audrey felt about leaving her cat behind.

While her parents were getting ready, Audrey went next door and spoke with Mrs. Orosco, giving her some last-minute instructions. "Midnight loves having his belly rubbed, but only if he's on the floor or the couch, not in your arms, otherwise he squirms and bites just enough to let you know he doesn't like that," Audrey explained. "And please keep his treats in the cupboard. If you leave them out, he'll find them and eat them all."

"Don't worry, Audrey," said Mrs. Orosco. "I will take good care of him."

Ida and Bill were loading the car in the garage when Audrey returned. "Just a minute," she told them. "I want to say good-bye to Midnight one more time." She hustled into the house and called to her cat. Normally, he came when he heard his name, but sometimes he played deaf if he was in a comfy spot in the closet or behind the living room drapes. This was one of those times. She went from room to room, looking for him. Hearing her father honk the car horn, Audrey ran out to the garage and said, "I can't find Midnight."

"He's hiding someplace," Ida said. "Maybe he's sulking because he knows we're going away."

"But what if he got out . . ."

"Audrey, Midnight is fine," Bill said. "He's a house cat who doesn't like being outside. He's probably sound asleep under the bed. Now get in. If we fool around here any longer, we'll miss our flight."

On the plane, Audrey sat by the window and stared at the changing landscape below. She knew she should be brimming with excitement about this holiday vacation, but she couldn't get Midnight out of her mind. *What if he got outside, and he's meowing in the cold and wants to get back in? What if he's sick and that's why he didn't come when I called him? What if he jumped into the dryer again? Oh, why didn't I look inside it?*

She thought back to the day they adopted him from the shelter. She was five years old, and he was the friskiest kitten in a litter that had been abandoned. As soon as she saw the all-black Siamese, she fell instantly in love with him.

I wish I could hold him right now. I wish he was flying with us to Auntie El's.

After they landed in New York, they were greeted in the airport baggage area by a uniformed driver for a car service arranged by Eleanor to pick up the family.

The driver was holding up a sign that read MISS AUDREY RODENBACH. Ida turned to Audrey and said, "Leave it to Auntie El to give you the star treatment."

On the ride to the apartment, Audrey badgered her mother into phoning Mrs. Orosco. "Hello, Mrs. Orosco? Hi, it's Ida. . . . Fine, thank you. . . . So, how is Midnight? . . . Uh-huh . . . Oh, dear . . . And you've looked everywhere? . . . The garage, the basement . . . Uh-huh . . . I see, even inside the washer and dryer? Well, sometimes he likes to hide. . . . No, I don't think so. . . . If he did sneak outside, he'd stay close to the house. . . ."

Listening to her mother's side of the conversation, Audrey became increasingly distressed. Squirming in her seat, she muttered, "I knew we should have brought him."

"Well, please go ahead and put fresh food in his dish, Mrs. Orosco," Ida said. "Then, if you wouldn't mind, return later tonight and check the dish. If the food is gone — and Midnight loves to eat — then we know he's all right. . . . Yes, and meanwhile, please tell the neighbors to be on the lookout for him, just in the remote chance . . ."

Audrey didn't hear the rest of the conversation. She was crying.

By the time the car reached the Park Avenue apartment building, Audrey had wiped away her tears. She wanted to put on a happy face for her great-aunt.

Eleanor Fontenot — the sister of Ida's mother — had no children of her own. Because Ida was her only niece, Eleanor had forged a strong relationship with her and eventually with Audrey. Eleanor was a bubbly, cheerful 57-year-old patron of the arts who lived life to the fullest. She counted among her close friends some of New York's highly acclaimed artists and sculptors, Broadway actors, opera stars, and jazz musicians. If there was a reception for a new gallery exhibit or the opening night of a musical, Eleanor most likely was in attendance. Her extravagantly furnished apartment reflected her taste in modern art, exquisite blown glass, and inventive metal sculptures. A gleaming grand piano, which she played skillfully, dominated the living room. Most of the walls that weren't covered by artwork were holding floor-to-ceiling shelves filled with hardcover books.

Eleanor was noted for wearing bright, flowing caftans and matching turbans. Her round, wrinkle-free face was framed in a treasure trove of necklaces and large dangling earrings handcrafted by her artisan friends.

With her infectious laugh, booming voice, and outgoing personality, Eleanor was anything but a wallflower.

The building's doorman personally escorted Audrey and her parents up to the fifth-floor apartment. When Eleanor opened the door, she spread out her arms and bellowed, "There she is . . . the princess of Indiana . . . Her Majesty Audrey Rodenbach!"

Forgetting about her missing cat, Audrey shouted, "Auntie El!" and rushed into the woman's ample, bracelet-filled arms. After smothering Audrey in kisses and embracing Ida and Bill, Eleanor stepped back, sized up the dimple-cheeked girl, and declared, "You're so pretty you belong on the cover of an American Girl book!"

But on second look, Eleanor noticed her bloodshot eyes. "Audrey? Have you been crying?"

Audrey nodded, and as the tears began to pool in her big brown eyes, she explained why she was upset.

"I have great faith that Midnight will show up," Eleanor declared. "Christmas is the season of faith, you know. And faith makes all things possible." Clapping her hands to change the subject, she said, "Now then, put your suitcases in your rooms. You'll unpack later. We're going to this quaint Italian restaurant and then attending the Radio City Christmas Spectacular. Christmas in

New York isn't really Christmas until you see the Rockettes."

At the restaurant, Audrey picked at her ricotta-and-spinach ravioli, still concerned about her missing cat. Mrs. Orosco had called back to report that after she'd left all the closets and room doors open, there was still no sign of Midnight. At Radio City Music Hall, Audrey tried to enjoy the amazing precision-dance company's performance, but her mind kept drifting back to her cat. Still, there were moments when she was fascinated by the Rockettes, especially when the 36 dancers formed a chorus line and did their famous eye-high leg kick in perfect unison.

When the family returned to the apartment, Audrey was mentally and physically exhausted and ready for bed. She went into her room and opened her suitcase to get out her pajamas. As she reached in, she saw something black and furry that she hadn't packed. She cautiously reached down and touched it and jerked away when it moved and then meowed.

"Midnight!" she shrieked. She picked him up and clutched him to her chest. "Midnight, oh, Midnight! I can't believe it's you!"

Her screams of delight brought Ida, Bill, and Eleanor rushing into the room, where they looked in amazement at the stowaway cat. Midnight was shaking uncontrollably from the trauma of being trapped in a suitcase for more than ten hours.

"Well, merry Christmas to you, Midnight!" Eleanor declared. "How's that for a present, Audrey?"

The family determined that Midnight had jumped into Audrey's open suitcase earlier in the morning and curled up on her black sweater. The girl hadn't noticed the cat when she closed the suitcase. The poor cat had remained inside the luggage during the hour-long car ride to the airport, the two-hour flight in the plane's cargo hold, the transfer from the plane to the baggage carousel, and the hours the suitcase was left unattended in the apartment.

"Auntie El, I am so sorry about this," Ida said.

"Nonsense," replied Eleanor. Then she added, "This is . . . ahem . . . very a-*mews*-ing. I can't wait to tell my friends."

When Audrey set Midnight down, the wide-eyed cat was still so freaked out that he streaked around the room before hiding under the bed and didn't come out until the morning. By then, Eleanor had already arranged for the delivery of a litter box, litter, cat food, cat treats, a water bowl, and a food bowl. It took the rest of the day for Midnight to settle down and begin purring again.

For his own well-being and to protect Eleanor's pricey furniture and lavishly decorated Christmas tree, he was kept in Audrey's bedroom.

Free from worrying about her cat, Audrey absorbed all the wonders that Christmastime in New York had to offer. She marveled at the fantastic department-store window displays at Bergdorf Goodman, Bloomingdale's, Saks Fifth Avenue, and Lord & Taylor. She skated at the famed Rockefeller Center ice rink, attended New York City Ballet's production of *The Nutcracker*, ogled at Macy's magical Santaland, and tap-danced on the giant floor piano at FAO Schwarz, America's oldest and most famous toy store.

On Christmas Day, Audrey opened several presents from Eleanor, including a hand-painted jacket, imported leather gloves, and a laptop. Eleanor even had a gift for Midnight — a cat carrier for the flight back to Indiana. Inside was his plane ticket so he could fly in the cabin and not the cargo hold.

The day before the family's departure, Bill and Ida went to breakfast with friends while Audrey and Eleanor stayed back. Audrey was playing on her bed with Midnight when she heard the doorbell. Eleanor called out, "Audrey, I'm on the phone. Please answer the door. It'll be the assistant doorman with a package for me."

Rather than leave the cat in her room, Audrey held him against her shoulder and walked to the door. She opened it and took a lightweight box from the man. At that moment, Mrs. Hildebrand from apartment 5-C was strolling by with her white-and-brown fox terrier, Zelda.

When the dog saw the cat, she barked. Midnight panicked, leaped off Audrey, and dashed down the hallway with the growling dog chasing after him. At the end of the hall, when it looked like Midnight was cornered, the crazed cat reared on his hind legs and swatted Zelda's nose with his left front paw. As the dog yelped in pain, Midnight took off again, streaking toward the other end of the hallway, past Audrey, the assistant doorman, and Mrs. Hildebrand, who were all shouting at the animals to stop.

It just so happened that a plumber had opened a hole in the wall of the hallway to fix a pipe. When he saw Zelda bearing down on the frantic cat, the plumber tried to block the dog. Looking for a place to hide, Midnight saw the opening, scurried through the plumber's legs, and jumped into the hole.

"Nooo!" cried Audrey. When the yelling and screaming from the others subsided, the plumber aimed a flashlight down into the hole. "I can't see anything," he reported. "This vent goes all the way to the basement — that's six flights."

Audrey rushed to the opening and shouted, "Midnight! Midnight! Say something!" She strained to hear any kind of meow but was met with silence. "He's hurt or he's dead!" she wailed.

Eleanor, who had come into the hall after hearing the commotion, led the distraught girl back into the apartment and tried to console her. "Your cat is a survivor," Eleanor told her. "He's proven that time and again, so don't give up on him yet. Let me see what I can do."

Eleanor made several calls and within an hour had a team of workers attempt a rescue through the basement wall. Using a drill, an electric saw, and an acetylene torch, they broke open the wall to the vent. But Midnight wasn't there.

Thinking that the cat might have landed on a ledge higher up, Eleanor persuaded Mrs. Ayers, a tenant on the first floor, to let workers drill a hole in her kitchen wall. The woman agreed only after Eleanor offered to pay for the damages.

Unfortunately, even that effort failed to find the cat. By then, Audrey was convinced that Midnight was dead. She sobbed. "I wish I were home," she blurted. "I wish I had never come to New York, because Midnight would still be alive!"

"Have faith and hope, princess," Eleanor stressed.

"I have both, because there's no proof that Midnight is dead, so I'm not quitting until we find him."

Eleanor approached Mr. Kemper, the owner of the second-floor apartment directly above Mrs. Ayers's, and explained the situation. Mr. Kemper was a grumpy elderly man, so it came as no surprise to Eleanor when he responded, "Are you crazy? You want workers to drill through my marble bathroom? Absolutely not."

"I will pay for all damages," countered Eleanor. "The life of a young child's cat is at stake!"

"It's just a cat," he muttered.

Audrey stepped around Eleanor and said, "Sir, he's my cat. And I need him back. Please, sir." She began crying again.

Eleanor clasped her hand on Mr. Kemper's shoulder and said softly, "It's Christmas. I have always thought of the holidays as a good time — a kind, generous time when people open their hearts freely." Then, in a low but firm voice, she said, "Mr. Kemper, open your heart!"

The man folded his arms and huffed. "Oh, all right," he said.

The workers carefully chiseled out a two-foot-by-two-foot slab of marble. Then, while one worker maneuvered a mirror into the hole, another one aimed his flashlight in the darkness. "I see him! I see him!" the worker announced. "He's alive!"

The workers needed to remove another marble slab before they could reach in and pull out Midnight. Other than some scrapes, the frightened cat seemed okay. As one of the workers handed the quivering cat to Audrey, he said, "Merry Christmas, little lady."

"Oh, thank you! Thank you!" she blubbered while squeezing her cat tightly.

Eleanor clapped her hands. "How wonderful is this! See, Audrey? Hope and faith."

Two days after the family returned home, Audrey received a package from Aunt Eleanor. When she opened the box, there was a handwritten note that read:

My darling Audrey:
I trust your cat caused no further turmoil on your return flight. I don't know whether my pocketbook could afford another feline predicament. (Just kidding! Midnight's survival and the look on your face when he was rescued were

worth every penny.) In all the excitement, I forgot about the package that the assistant doorman had given you, which started the near calamity. The package was from a talented artist and dear friend of mine from the south of France. This is a unique sculpted filigreed metal angel that he made for me for Christmas. However, when I saw what he engraved on its base, I knew immediately that in light of your cat's misadventure, you should have it.

All my love,
Auntie El

Audrey reached into a mound of Styrofoam peanuts and pulled out a shiny abstract angel. On the base were the words "Christmas reminds us that hope is never lost, and faith is everywhere."

TANGO'S CHRISTMAS MIRACLE

When Lorena Ruiz-Torres came home from the grocery store, she opened the front door and yelped in surprise at the unexpected condition of her living room. Christmas pillows from the couch were piled in a corner. Wooden Santas from the coffee table were perched on chairs. Holiday candles were strewn on the couch. And more than a dozen tree ornaments were scattered on the floor.

"Somebody has been redecorating the house," she said in a lighthearted voice. Off to her left, Lorena spotted a small, elf-like face peeking from behind the curtains of a bay window. "Tango? Did you do this?"

A two-foot-tall, white-faced capuchin monkey

emerged, chattering happily. He bounded onto a chair and then leaped onto her shoulder, where he reached into her bag of groceries and pulled out a jicama, a sweet Mexican turnip-like vegetable. Grabbing the jicama from him, she said, "No, Tango. That's for Christmas brunch tomorrow."

Walking into the kitchen, she said, "Now do you see why I didn't put the presents under the tree? You would have opened them all." She set the groceries down and then lifted him off her shoulder. Holding him in front of her, she asked Tango, "How in the world did you get out of your cage, you naughty little boy? I know I locked it before I left."

The monkey was usually kept in a large eight-foot-tall cage in an empty bedroom whenever Lorena and her husband, Enrique Torres, were either out of the house or asleep. The rest of the time, Tango had the run of the place.

With Tango back on her shoulders and playing with her long black hair, Lorena went into the monkey's room to investigate. The padlock was open and dangling from the latch of the cage door.

"How did you open it without the key?" she asked him. "Or did you steal it?"

He leaped into his cage, picked up a favorite toy, a

rubber ducky, and squeezed it. He wasn't going to tell her anything.

Lorena thought back to earlier in the morning when she had unlocked the cage. She remembered that he had jumped into her arms and given her a big hug. Wanting to hug him back, she had dropped the key into the pocket of her robe.

"Tango, if the key is not in my robe, then I know you are a clever little pickpocket," she said. She went into her bathroom and checked the pockets. The key wasn't there. She returned to the monkey's room and, in mock anger, said, "You sneaky thief! When you were hugging me this morning, you stole the key from my pocket and waited until I left to open your cage. What did you do with my key?"

He ignored her.

"I know where to look," she told him. She entered his cage and lifted his pillow, revealing the key. "Aha!" she exclaimed, holding it up in triumph. Finding it hard to scold such an intelligent animal, she uttered a feeble "Shame on you, Tango." Still grasping the rubber ducky, he jumped into her arms again and whimpered — his way of acknowledging that, yes, he had misbehaved. She gave him a hug and kissed him on his head. "I can't stay mad at you, Tango. No one can."

Then she noticed his eyes didn't have their usual sparkle. His easy-to-read face had a sad, wistful look, much like it had when she first met him years earlier.

"You miss Papi, don't you? We all do."

Twelve-year-old Lorena Ruiz skipped through the aisles of the flea market, her sneakers kicking up the red Arizona dust. "Papi," she called out to her father, Carlos, "I'll be in the back with the animals."

Just beyond the tents that held all the knickknack-laden tables, a fenced-in area contained a "poor man's" zoo of unwanted animals for sale — swaybacked horses, yapping puppies, mewing kittens, squawking chickens, and assorted geckos, iguanas, and snakes. Lorena petted as many of the animals as she could, wishing that each would find a good home. In fact, it was here that she convinced her mother, Camilla, a year earlier to buy two kittens from a man who claimed they had been abandoned.

Lorena's eyes landed on a rickety chicken-wire cage in the back of a rusted-out pickup truck. Inside, a sorrowful-looking, small, white-faced capuchin paced aimlessly. It was a breed best known for performing with organ-grinders and clowns. The monkey scratched the top of his head, which had a crown of black hair that reminded Lorena of the skullcaps worn by monks. His long, curled tail was pencil-thin, his brown coat dull and patchy.

The girl approached him slowly until the two made eye contact. "Hello, monkey," she said softly. The animal moved closer, stared at her, and then extended a bony arm through the cage wire. Lorena held out her hand and let the capuchin wrap his tiny fingers around her index finger. The girl, who had never touched a monkey before, noticed that his hand looked like that of a human baby. Her heart melted.

"What's his name?" she asked the owner, a bald, stubble-bearded man who was playing dominoes on a portable table with a cigar-chomping white-haired woman.

The man squinted and replied, "Tango. He's four months old. He'll make a nice pet for you, *niña bonita*."

The woman took the cigar out of her mouth and added, "He'll eat anything except habaneros [spicy chili peppers]." She cackled. "Never heard a monkey howl like that."

Snickering, the man added, "Remember how *loco* he was when I gave him Tabasco sauce to drink?"

"How awful," Lorena muttered under her breath.

The monkey kept his gaze on the girl, who tried to read his eyes. *He looks scared*, she thought. *He looks abused. Is he begging me to buy him?*

The monkey was still holding on to Lorena's finger when her father walked up. "Did you make a new *amigo*?" he asked her. Carlos, a longtime animal lover, studied the capuchin. "*Hola, monito* [little monkey]. How are you?" The monkey released his grip on Lorena and grasped Carlos's finger.

"Papi, please, can we buy him?" she begged. "Let him be my Christmas present. I won't ask for anything else."

"I've always wanted to have a capuchin," Carlos admitted. Seeing the monkey's poor physical condition — his belly was extended, indicating he was malnourished — Carlos made a rash decision. "How much?" he asked the bald man.

After some haggling, they agreed on a price that pretty much cleaned out Carlos's wallet. As Carlos picked up the cage, he told Lorena, "*Mija*, this is an early Christmas present for the family. Won't Mama be surprised?"

From that day on, Tango was a loving — and loved — member of the Ruiz family.

He immediately formed attachments to Lorena and her father, and less quickly to her mother, who needed a couple of days to get over the shock of a monkey living in the house. Camilla, a dental hygienist, was also an animal lover and eventually developed a warm relationship with him. Even the cats learned to accept him.

Tango's life became far different from that of his fellow capuchins in the wild. They lived in trees in the low-lying rain forests of Central and South America. Tango slept in a large cage in the office at home where Carlos worked as a translator of technical journals and manuals. Wild capuchins foraged for ripe fruit, vegetation, nuts, flowers, seeds, roots, insects, spiders, and snails. Tango was bottle-fed milk and given store-bought fruits and vegetables, fortified monkey chow, and human food and was allowed to eat at the dinner table. Monkeys in the forests pooped wherever they wanted. Tango wore diapers. His fellow capuchins could expect to live 20 to 25 years in the wild. Tango had a life expectancy in captivity of 35 to 40 years.

The monkey had fun playing with Lorena and enjoyed cuddle time with Camilla. But Carlos was his favorite. The two formed a close relationship, partly because Carlos (whom Tango knew only as Papi) worked at home and spent the most time with him. Papi also pampered him.

In the first few weeks, the monkey snuggled in Papi's lap while Papi worked at his computer. This arrangement wasn't without its perils. At the most inopportune times, Tango would leap onto the desk and start tapping on the keyboard, ruining the sentence or paragraph Papi was translating. To Papi's great annoyance, the monkey pressed the computer's "off" button on several occasions.

As long as someone was home, Tango was allowed most anywhere. He spent his early days exploring jewelry boxes, desk drawers, kitchen cupboards, and bedroom closets. The monkey was more than an explorer, however. He was also a thief who habitually swiped items and hid them. Lorena lost count of the missing earrings and bracelets that turned up in the oddest places, such as the sugar bowl and the toothbrush holder.

Sometimes Tango took an item and left another object in its place. In Lorena's jewelry box, for instance, a ring or a watch would be replaced by a stone, a paper clip, or a battery. Many things appeared where they didn't belong. Lorena found her favorite pen atop the toilet, the TV remote in her underwear drawer, and her sunglasses in the kitchen garbage can.

The family had to install baby-proof locks on drawers and cabinets, trying to stem Tango's mischievous ways. But it was impossible to secure everything, so the monkey still created annoying moments for them, like when he hid car keys.

On nice days, Lorena put a harness and leash on Tango and took him for walks. He was a neighborhood celebrity. In a common antic that always brought a laugh, he would snatch a kid's baseball cap and stick it on his own head. Naturally, the hat would be too big for him and cover his eyes. Unable to see, he would stagger around with his arms outstretched like a blindfolded person.

He was a prankster at home. One time, Lorena was vacuuming the living room when the machine quit. As she walked toward the electrical outlet, which was out of her line of sight behind the couch, the vacuum roared to life. She resumed her chore until the machine stopped a second time. Once again, she headed toward the outlet only to hear the vacuum go on. She thought, *Either there's a short or* . . . She tiptoed to the couch and then peered behind it. There was Tango, who had been pulling the cord out and plugging it back in. "I caught you, you little sneak!" she shouted.

The monkey laughed, scooted out of the room, ran into the office, and jumped on Papi's lap. That was Tango's sanctuary, his safe haven from the consequences of his troublemaking. No matter how irritated the monkey made Lorena or Camilla, Papi protected him. In his cheerful, easygoing manner, Papi simmered them down and showed them how funny Tango's latest caper was.

No one could remain angry at Tango. He was just too cute and lovable.

The capuchin was Lorena's "monkey brother." He made her giggle when she was mad, calmed her when she was tense, consoled her when she was sad. But as Lorena grew older, she began spending more time with her girlfriends. By high school, she was focused on soccer and boys. Then she left home to attend college, married Enrique Torres, an accountant, and became a medical transcriptionist.

Although she had her own life as an adult, Lorena saw her parents and Tango quite often, because she lived only a few miles away. The monkey always greeted her with a hug around the neck and a toothy smile.

Shortly after Tango's sixteenth birthday, which was in October, the newlyweds moved into their new house. They were still unpacking when Lorena received a call that dropped her to her knees. "Papi was in a terrible accident," Camilla said. "He's in the emergency room right now."

"Dios mío!" cried Lorena. "What happened?"

"Papi was outside building a bigger enclosure for Tango on the patio when he fell off the ladder and struck his head on a boulder. He lost consciousness, and when he came to, he suffered a seizure. *Mija*, it's bad!"

"Oh, poor Papi! I'm on my way."

At the hospital, Lorena and Camilla tearfully embraced and began pacing in the waiting room. "Tango saw the whole thing from the porch," said Camilla. "He was so upset. He was shrieking and ran into the house. I didn't know what had happened. I followed him out to the porch and found Papi lying in a pool of blood on the patio."

An hour later, the doctor told them, "Carlos has suffered a serious head injury. We had to perform surgery to remove clotted blood that was putting pressure on the brain. It will take days to assess just how much brain damage he sustained."

The injury turned out to be worse than the family had feared. Papi couldn't talk and could barely move his left arm and leg. Eventually, he was transferred to a rehabilitation center, where a team of therapists tried to help him relearn basic skills, such as walking and talking.

Camilla was seldom home anymore, because she was spending her days at work and her evenings at the rehab center, so Lorena took Tango to live with her and Enrique. Lorena even received permission from her boss to work part-time at home to spend time with her father and take better care of the monkey.

She and Enrique dismantled the cage in Papi's office and set it up in their new house in a spare, unfurnished bedroom. Having lived virtually all his life at one residence, Tango was a nervous wreck over the move, despite having his favorite toys and blanket — and stuffed animals Booboo and Baby, which he slept with every night. What Tango missed most, of course, was Papi. Lorena did her best to soothe the forlorn monkey, singing lullabies to him at night and feeding him extra treats.

She and Enrique monkey-proofed the kitchen and kept the doors to all the rooms closed to limit his temptation for mischief. It took about two weeks for Tango to begin dabbling in "monkey business." The couple found a missing watch in Enrique's tennis shoe; a baseball autographed by the Arizona Diamondbacks in the toilet; a chewed-up new roll of one hundred stamps in the laundry hamper; a torn grocery list on top of the refrigerator; and Enrique's college ring in a potted cactus.

When the couple brought home a Christmas tree and began decorating it, Tango had his own ideas of where the ornaments should go. Years of experience had taught Lorena not to use breakable decorations, so when he yanked off some ornaments or threw them, they wouldn't shatter.

Aside from these little bits of naughtiness, Tango was settling in to his new surroundings and remained the adorable, delightful monkey he had always been.

Papi, however, was having a difficult time in rehab. He had fallen into a deep depression and became combative and uncooperative. He communicated in grunts and grumbles, not words. Walking only with the assistance of a therapist, he put little effort into physical exercise. He barely ate, watched television, or showed any interest in reading. He was the opposite of the Carlos Ruiz whom everyone knew and loved. "He's lost his will to live," Camilla confided to Lorena. "He wants to wither up and die."

By mid-December, officials at the rehab center told Camilla there wasn't any more they could do for him unless he began to help himself. They said she had two choices: take him home or take him to an assisted-living facility. Camilla took a leave of absence from work and began caring for him at home. He wasn't talking or eating and used a wheelchair to get around.

Because Camilla had her hands full at home, Tango remained with Lorena and Enrique.

Eager to cheer up Papi, Lorena convinced Camilla to bring him over on Christmas Day. "He needs to see Tango," Lorena said. "That *monito* misses his Papi terribly, and I'm sure Papi misses him."

"It's worth a try," said Camilla. "If Tango can't get Papi to smile, then there's no hope. Just a smile from him. That's all I want for Christmas."

On Christmas Day, Lorena had prepared a brunch that she thought her father couldn't resist: *chilaquiles al horno*, a baked dish of shredded chicken, cheese, cream, and fried corn tortillas bathed in a fiery chili sauce; *arroz verde con queso y rajas*, green rice casserole with poblano chilis and cheese; *ensalada xec*, jicama and mandarin orange salad; and *rompope*, Puebla-style eggnog.

The holiday decorations were back where they were supposed to be after Tango's rearrangement, and all the ornaments remained on the tree, other than a bright green one that the monkey rolled down the hallway. A friend had made a tiny Christmas outfit for Tango — a Santa hat and a red coat with white trim and matching pants.

Enrique drove to the Ruiz house and helped Camilla get Papi and his wheelchair into the car. On the trip, Papi remained silent, although Camilla sensed that he was looking forward to seeing Tango. When they arrived, Enrique wheeled Papi into the living room by the Christmas tree.

"*Feliz Navidad*, Papi!" said Lorena, planting a big kiss on his unshaven cheek. He nodded. Seeing his eyes dart around the room, she said, "Are you looking for Tango? Just a minute and let me get him."

Moments earlier, she had put Tango in her bedroom, where she planned to dress him in the Santa outfit before leading him out to the living room for the reunion with the human he loved — and missed — most.

She walked down the hallway and froze. Waddling out of the master bedroom came Tango, covered from head to toe in talcum powder. His face was crisscrossed with ruby-red lipstick and black eyeliner. His chest was coated with rouge and his lips were smeared with white hand lotion. Holding a white bath towel on top of his head so it draped down his back like a long head scarf, Tango scurried into the living room.

He chattered in his usual goofy, nonsensical way while doing a little dance, sending Lorena, Enrique, and Camilla into fits of laughter. Suddenly, above the hysterics, they heard Papi roar, "Tango! Tango! You silly *monito*!" The words were a little slurred but easily understandable. He began to chortle, then guffaw, and within seconds, he was doubled up in laughter in his wheelchair.

Hearing him laugh and speak a complete sentence for the first time since the accident, the others stopped giggling and gasped in amazement.

Tango had been so caught up in his high jinks that he hadn't even noticed Papi at first. But once he heard Papi's voice, the monkey tossed the towel aside and leaped into his lap. Papi's loud laughter evolved into hard sobs. "Oh, Tango, I missed you so much!" He bent over, kissing the makeup-wearing monkey on his powdered head. Papi held him tight, not only with his right arm but with his left arm, the one he could barely move since the accident.

By now, everyone in the room — including Tango — was having a good cry, a happy cry. This moment had turned into more than an emotional reunion; it had transformed into a physical and mental breakthrough for Papi. He spoke; he laughed; he moved his left arm. The depression that had virtually paralyzed him was lifting.

In that instant, Lorena knew that her father had taken the first step on the road to recovery, that his will to live had been revived, that he would do everything he could to return to his old self. "Papi, you're back!" she declared.

"Yes, I'm back," he said, grinning.

Once the euphoria died down, Lorena gazed at that nutty painted-up monkey and chuckled. Then it dawned on her: "My bathroom!"

She ran into the room and shrieked, not so much in horror as in hilarity. "Everyone, come here!" she shouted. "You have to see this!"

Camilla, Enrique, and Papi, who was still holding Tango, crowded by the bathroom doorway and shared another hearty laugh at the scene: Spilled containers of lotion, powder, and makeup lay on the counter. Lipstick was scrawled on the mirror, powder covered the floor, toilet paper was draped over the sink and bathtub, and handprints of makeup and rouge blotted the walls.

"How did he get in here?" Lorena said. "The door was closed."

"I think I know," said Enrique. "Yesterday I saw him hanging on to the doorknob, swinging left and right, trying to get it open. He couldn't do it. Obviously, today he succeeded."

"Look at Tango," she said, pointing to the monkey, who was chirping and hopping up and down on Papi's lap. "He's proud of himself for this mess." She went to him and kissed him. "You crazy monkey!" Turning to the others, she said, "I'll clean it up later. Let's go eat!"

At brunch, Lorena beamed with satisfaction at seeing her father eating well for the first time in weeks. Tango ate from his own plate at the dinner table while rooted in Papi's lap.

After the meal, Enrique wheeled Papi into the living room to watch football on TV. Minutes later, Enrique came into the kitchen, where Lorena and Camilla were doing the dishes. He whispered to the women, "Follow me."

In the living room, Papi and Tango were sound asleep in the wheelchair. Papi's arms were wrapped around the monkey, who was snuggled on his chest.

"This is a sight to behold," said Camilla.

"It's more than that, Mama," said Lorena. "This is a Christmas miracle."

THE GIFT HORSE

Every year since she was old enough to spell, Penelope "Penny" Randle wrote the same thing at the top of her Christmas list: a horse of her own.

She lived and breathed horses, even though her parents and two older brothers had no interest in or experience with the animals other than the occasional guided trail ride in the Kentucky hills near their home. Penny eventually understood that her parents — Arnie, a deputy sheriff, and Susan, a massage therapist — couldn't afford a horse, let alone keep one in their small backyard in the middle of town. No, the best they could do for Penny's Christmas gifts was pay for her riding lessons and give her horse statues, stuffed horses, books about horses, DVDs about horses, and horse-themed novels. She never complained that her number one wish was out of reach; she was grateful for any present that made her feel a part of the horse world.

In the winter after Penny turned 13, the Randles moved to the country. To her unbridled joy, their property was near Blue Ridge Stables, a horse farm that offered boarding services, training, and riding lessons. Yearning to be with the horses, she asked Blue Ridge owners Hale and Beverly Conroy for a part-time job, but they didn't need another stable girl.

The lure of the horses was just too strong for the tall, gangly teen. Often around dusk, she would sneak over to the paddock and ride a gray Welsh pony bareback without anyone knowing about it. On these secret rides, Penny was not the shy, gawky girl who towered over, and sometimes tripped over, the boys in her class. She was a confident, fluid horsewoman. All the cares of the world — well, all the worries and angst of a typical teenage girl — vanished in the wind. This was heaven.

But one foggy evening, Hale nabbed Penny as she hopped off the pony. Furious that she was trespassing and riding someone else's horse without permission — and without a helmet! — he read her the riot act. But he softened when she poured out her heart describing her passion for horses. She ended with another pitch to work as a stable girl, and this time Hale agreed.

As part of her job, Penny was allowed to ride and exercise certain horses.

So most days after school and on weekends, she put her blond hair into a ponytail and happily mucked out stables, swept alleyways, and cleaned tack. She didn't mind manure on her boots, hay in her hair, and sawdust up her nose, because she was where she wanted to be. With Spirit, Marigold, Cream Soda, Gypsy, Olive Oyl, Windrunner, and Buckshot, to name a few. True, they were other people's horses. But that didn't stop her from falling in love with them all, even the older lesson horses, such as Beau and Beauty.

Penny didn't know what to think about Fireball. A four-year-old sorrel quarter horse with a flaxen mane, he was a "rescue" from a Lexington farm that had gone bankrupt. Fireball was a physical and mental wreck when he arrived at Blue Ridge Stables. Unlike others of his breed, he didn't have toned muscles, and his rounded hindquarters were sunken. "I suspect he was abused," Beverly told Penny as he was being led out of the horse trailer. "He's an angry, nervous cuss. And he spooks easily." Penny went to him and tried to pet his short, refined head, but he shied away. His twitching ears, flaring nostrils, and bugged-out eyes showed he wanted nothing to do with her. She backed off, upset because she had always enjoyed good rapport with the other horses. "He's afraid of me," Penny complained.

"He's afraid of everyone," said Beverly. "We're going to have to gain his trust slowly by loving him and caring for him. It won't be easy."

Because of Fireball's fear of people, the stable hands were careful and tender with him. Penny took turns sitting in a lawn chair next to a bucket of grain and stroked the side of his face when he ate. It sometimes took a half hour for Fireball to eat the grain, because he backed off each time she touched him. During this tedious process, she sweet-talked him, telling him he was safe, he was beautiful, and he was loved.

In return, he sometimes — probably deliberately — stepped on her foot or blew mucus on her shirt. He had an uncanny knack for swatting his ample tail whenever Penny was grooming his hindquarters, leaving her with red marks on her cheeks.

Fireball wasn't anyone's favorite horse, but Penny and the trainers showed him the compassion he needed. Thanks to their persistence and patience, the horse filled out nicely, so Beverly and Hale began training him to become a lesson horse. However, his intelligence was overshadowed by his ornery attitude, so he often balked at the simplest commands. His pinched mouth, narrow eyes, swishing tail, and strained neck indicated he was in no mood to cooperate.

Although there were days throughout the spring when he caused no problems for riders, he still reacted wildly whenever he was spooked, which was fairly often. He had thrown every Blue Ridge instructor and stable hand at least once, with one exception — Penny. But she didn't own those bragging rights for long.

One muggy afternoon following a rain, Penny was supposed to walk Fireball in from the back paddock. Because she was feeling lazy, she hopped on his bare back and, with a halter and rope, leisurely rode him toward the gate. Seeing Fireball, the other horses in the field thought it was time to go in and started galloping. Suddenly, he took off, too. Surprised, Penny felt herself slipping, so she instinctively pressed her legs extra hard against his sides. The horse didn't appreciate this and bucked like a bronco, launching her over his head. Penny landed on the down side of a slight slope, belly first, and had the wind knocked out of her. With her arms extended like Superman's, she skidded on the wet grass, arriving at the gate a second or two before he did. The stable hands who witnessed the feat doubled over in hysterics. Even Fireball looked like he was laughing.

Once she caught her breath, Penny lurched to her feet and tried flicking the mud and muck off her clothes. She didn't bother cleaning her face, because the yucky stuff hid the flush of embarrassment on her cheeks. Penny walked stiff-legged over to Fireball and said, "That wasn't nice."

The horse neighed.

"He's just a jerk, and always will be," said a stable hand.

Penny shook her head. "He'll make a good horse . . . someday."

Everyone knew Fireball was smart. He learned to unlatch his stall door by putting his tongue between the upper door and the frame to pop the hook out of the eye bolt, then lifting the latch on the outside of the lower door with his lips. He also figured out that thunderstorms often disabled the electric fence. So after a storm, he would approach the fence slowly, feeling for vibrations on his nose hairs. If he didn't detect any, he would push down the fence and explore the area. Twice while bicycling to the farm, Penny found him trotting alone down the road in the opposite direction.

Sometimes when she called him in the pasture, he ignored her, making her trudge a hundred or so yards to where he was grazing. "Oh, is your hearing going bad?" she sarcastically said to him after the third time he did that to her. "I've got news for you. I've seen your future — dog food!"

He got even for her mocking the next day. Penny had removed her jacket and draped it over the fence. In an unguarded moment, Fireball picked up the jacket with his teeth and galloped off to the far corner of the paddock. When Penny recovered her jacket, she found it covered in hoofprints, an obvious sign that he had stomped on it.

Fireball was at his best during longeing, a training technique in which the horse is at the end of a long line and responds to a handler who is standing in the middle of a big circle. Every time Penny caught a glimpse of one of his sessions, she thought he looked content. His reddish-brown coat glistened under his golden mane.

Although Penny spent more time riding other horses, she was growing increasingly comfortable with Fireball. She felt drawn to him despite his horseplay.

One of her riding companions was Claire Taylor, a 16-year-old who looked like a slightly pudgy version of a young Britney Spears. Claire's divorced father showered her with expensive gifts — the lipstick-red Ford Mustang being the latest. Because she was fairly new to riding, her father promised to buy her a horse once she became a better horsewoman. To her credit, Claire didn't flaunt her wealth and was down to earth. Even though she was older than Penny and came from a different background, the two enjoyed each other's company and occasionally rode together.

With Penny on Fireball and Claire on Gypsy, the girls headed into the woods on a hot summer day and talked about their love of horses.

"Which horse is your favorite?" Claire asked.

"I love them all," Penny answered. "Kizzy and Ebony are the easiest to ride, and I have fun on Calypso because he loves to gallop. Lately, I've been spending time with this guy here," she said, patting Fireball. "I'm growing fond of him even though he causes me the most aggravation."

The trail led them deeper into the woods, where the only sounds were the clopping of hooves. As the girls passed several large trees downed by a recent storm, a helicopter overhead broke the silence of the forest.

Fireball, who was still easily spooked, reared up from the sudden noise. Penny leaned forward so she wouldn't fall off. "Steady, boy. Steady," she told him. While she tried to keep him under control, the unsettled horse reared again. Then he backed up into the crown of a big fallen tree, pinning Penny into the fork of a thick branch. Fireball gave a little kick and then charged forward. Caught in the fork under her armpits, Penny slipped off his back and was left dangling about four feet from the ground.

"Fireball! Get back here!" she commanded.

He stopped about ten yards ahead and looked back in surprise that his rider was no longer on him. Meanwhile, Claire burst out laughing at seeing her friend suspended in the tree. As Penny wriggled to free herself, the fork broke and she dropped to the ground. By now, Claire was laughing so hard that she could barely stay atop Gypsy.

Dusting herself off, Penny laughed, too. "Oh, when will Fireball get his act together?"

Still giggling, Claire said, "That has to be the funniest fall off a horse I've ever seen."

"That does *not* count as a fall," Penny claimed. "I fell out of a tree, not off a horse."

That night, Penny complained to her mother, Susan, about a sharp pain that extended from her shoulder to her lower back. Relying on her therapy training, Susan diagnosed the problem as a pinched nerve and gave her several deep massages, until the pain went away.

A few days later, Penny was giving Fireball a bath. When she used a sweat scraper to remove the water from his back, he stomped his foot, turned his head, and glared at her. "Oh, is your back hurting?" Penny said. "Hmmm. Maybe you have a pinched nerve." She began examining his back with her fingers, pressing hard at various points. He whinnied and stepped away whenever she exerted force on a spot where the weight from a saddle would be at its greatest.

Then came her "aha" moment. "Now it all makes sense to me," she told him. "You seem much happier and more cooperative when we work with you without the saddle. When someone rides you, the saddle makes your pain worse, and so you misbehave and become stubborn and difficult. It's not because you have a bad attitude. It's because you're hurting. All this time you've been trying to tell us you've been suffering, and no one — me included — has been listening to you. Well, I hear you now."

After Penny explained her theory to the Conroys, they brought in a veterinarian. He confirmed that Fireball had a pinched nerve, and prescribed some supplements and muscle relaxants. Susan came over and provided regular massages for the horse. At the vet's suggestion, no one was to ride Fireball for two weeks unless it was bareback.

By fall, Fireball had transformed into a different horse — one that was happy and relaxed. He was much more cooperative, following commands without his usual pigheaded behavior. He never deliberately threw another rider and he barely got spooked anymore.

But this huge change presented a dilemma for Penny. She was feeling closer to him than ever before because she understood him. Through that understanding, he was becoming a better horse, which meant everyone wanted to ride him.

Sure, she was attached to other horses, too — especially Kizzy and Calypso — but she now felt a stronger and deeper connection with Fireball. If she could have any horse, it would be him.

During dinner in early December, Penny told her parents, "Christmas is almost here, so you can guess what I want more than anything in the world."

"A horse, of course," her parents answered in unison.

"I know you can't afford to buy me a horse, but could we lease one? With the money I've saved and with your help, it could be affordable. It would be almost like having my own horse."

"But why would you want to lease a horse?" Susan asked. "You can ride most any horse at the stables for free."

"I know," Penny said. "But Fireball and I have a special bond. I love all the horses, but I love him more." She put down her fork. "I don't want any presents for Christmas. Just give me whatever money you had planned to spend for my gifts. Please, I want Fireball and I know he wants me."

After Penny spelled out the costs, her dad, Arnie, glanced at her mother, smiled, and said, "I think we can swing it."

Penny rocketed out of her chair and embraced her parents. "This is turning into the most fantastic Christmas of my life!" she said.

Early the next morning, Penny jumped on her bike and zoomed over to the stables. Out of breath when she reached the barn, she cornered Beverly and squealed, "Bev, Bev, guess what!"

"What is it, child?" the owner asked, smiling in anticipation of some apparently delightful development that was about to be revealed.

"I want to lease Fireball for the year. I have the money!"

Beverly's smile froze for a moment and then vanished. "Oh, honey . . ."

"We're a perfect match after all we've been through together. Sure, we have much more to learn, but one-on-one will make me a better rider and make him a better horse. And . . ." Penny had been jabbering with such enthusiasm that she hadn't noticed until that second that Beverly was wincing, and her eyes were watering. "Bev, what's the matter?"

Beverly put her arm around Penny's shoulder and said, "Let's sit down on the bench. I have something to tell you."

"Is Fireball all right?"

"Yes, he's fine. But I'm afraid you won't be after you hear what I say."

Penny gulped, grabbed Beverly's hand, and said, "You're scaring me. What is it?"

"There's no easy way to say this, honey." She hesitated, knowing that the next three words would break a young girl's heart. "We sold Fireball."

Penny felt like she had been kicked in the stomach by an enraged horse. No, worse. Much worse. Gagged by shock and grief, she couldn't speak. She wrapped her arms around her chest, dropped her head onto her knees, and sobbed.

"I am so, so sorry, honey," said Beverly, stroking the girl's hair. "I know the owners, and they will take very good care of him."

When Penny was finally able to talk, she looked up at Beverly and blubbered, "You mean, they're not going to board him here?"

"No. The owners are putting up a paddock and barn at their home. They should be ready by Christmas."

"Who bought him?"

Preparing herself for the explosion that was about to erupt, Beverly replied, "Claire's father. He owns twenty acres behind his house and —"

"Claire? Claire gets to own Fireball because Divorced Daddy Moneybags can buy her love?" Penny pounded the bench with her fists and let out an angry cry that caused the horses in the stables to whinny. "Claire? My friend Claire who has everything in the world, and now is getting the one thing — the only thing — that I ever wanted? Can life be any more unfair?"

As she stormed out of the stables, she heard Beverly say, "You can lease Kizzy or Calypso or . . ."

"I want Fireball!" Penny cried back. She was so upset that she didn't bother riding her bike back home. Instead, she ran through the paddock, past the grazing horses, into the open field to her house, crying all the way.

Flinging open the back door, she wailed, "Mom! They sold Fireball!" Without waiting for a response, she charged upstairs to her room and dived onto her bed. She clutched her favorite stuffed horse, buried her head in her pillow, and sobbed.

Feeling her mother's soft touch, Penny was in no mood to be comforted, and pulled in her shoulders. Then she turned over and lashed out. "Why couldn't you and Dad have bought him? You know how much I love him."

"And you know we can't afford a horse. Penny, you're distraught, and you have every right to feel that way. But you're such a horse lover that surely you'll be happy with one of the others that we can lease."

Penny shook her head. "No horse will ever replace Fireball!" As she flipped back onto her stomach, she said, "Let me grieve. Alone."

Within an hour her heartache morphed into rage. She called Claire and said, "Your dad bought Fireball for you?"

"Yes, isn't that wonderful?"

Shaking from fury, Penny snapped, "No, it's terrible! How could you do that to me?"

"What do you mean?" asked Claire, taken aback by her friend's angry tone.

"You knew I loved Fireball the most."

"No, I didn't. I knew you spent the most time with him, Penny, but you told me you loved all the horses you rode."

"He and I have a special connection. Why did you have to buy him?"

"Fireball has turned into a beautiful, sweet horse."

"He's not right for you. You ride with very heavy hands and a terribly bouncy seat. He needs someone with soft hands who reads his cues. He needs me!" Penny hung up before Claire could respond.

It took two weeks for Penny to release much of her sorrow and anger from losing Fireball. During that time, she decided to stay away from the stables. It hurt too much. When she finally came to terms with her disappointment, she apologized to her mother and Beverly for the meltdown. Penny also called Claire, said she was very sorry, and wished her good rides with Fireball.

On Christmas Day, Penny received some cash as well as new riding tights, riding gloves, and a helmet. "This has been a wonderful Christmas," she told her family after all the presents were opened.

"Have you picked out which horse you want to lease?" Arnie asked her.

"I've decided not to lease a horse," she replied. "I'll just get way too attached to a horse and then, before you know it, I'll be going away to college and . . . well . . . it's just better this way."

Later that morning, Beverly called and invited the family over for her famous cinnamon pecan coffee cake. Penny wanted to stay home but figured now was as good a time as any to cope with her first day back at Blue Ridge without Fireball.

When the family arrived, Beverly ushered everyone into the barn for some photos. She asked Penny, "Would you mind walking down to the stall just past Kizzy's? Having you stand under the shaft of light from the skylight over there will make an excellent picture."

As Penny strolled past the occupied stalls, she called out to Spirit and Marigold and rubbed the noses of Buckshot and Cream Soda. When she reached Kizzy's stall, she stopped and hugged the horse's neck. With her back to the next stall, Penny asked Beverly, "Would you please take a picture of me and Kizzy?"

"Sure," Beverly replied. After shooting a few frames, she said to Penny, "Okay, now still face me and take a couple of steps back. The light is better there."

Penny did what she was told. As she stood smiling, she felt a big wet nose nudge her in the neck. She wheeled around. For an instant, she wondered if her eyes were playing tricks on her. "Fireball!" she shouted in glee.

"You're still here!" She kissed him and pressed her face against his head.

By then everyone had crowded around the stall. To Penny's surprise, Claire and her father had joined the group. "Merry Christmas, Claire," said Penny. "I thought you were keeping Fireball at your dad's home. Are you going to board him here instead?"

Everyone started to snicker at Penny. "Look at the nameplate on the front of the stall door, and you'll understand," Claire replied.

Penny stepped back and examined the embossed metal sign on the door. It was the same kind that was affixed to all the other stalls of the horses, giving the names of the boarders and owners. This one read FIREBALL, OWNED BY PENNY RANDLE.

Penny covered her mouth with both hands, afraid the joy she was about to unleash would frighten the horses. She let loose with a volley of screams, followed by shouts, then shrieks. Then came the sobs. She bawled so hard that she collapsed into the arms of the nearest person, her father.

When Penny finally regained control of her emotions, she said, "He's . . . really . . . mine? . . . But . . . how?"

Claire stepped forward and said, "When you told me how upset you were that my dad had bought Fireball for me, I felt just awful. I couldn't sleep. Honestly, I didn't know he meant that much to you. So I called Beverly and asked her if we could buy Ebony instead. I've always enjoyed riding him, and we get along great."

Beverly picked up the story. "I saw how crushed you were about losing Fireball, and it tore me up. So Hale and I talked to your parents. We know how much you love all the horses here, and you've been a big help to us. Why, if it wasn't for you, Fireball might still be an unhappy, misbehaving horse. He's special, and you two deserve each other. So we've worked out a financial arrangement with your parents."

"Fireball is yours," said Arnie. "Merry Christmas, Penny!"

Laughing and crying at the same time, Penny blubbered, "Now I won't have to write 'horse' anymore at the top of my Christmas list!"

A HOLLY, JOLLY CHRISTMAS

There was hardly any talking during the Gerard family's five-hour drive from their home in San Jose, California, to their Christmas vacation rental in the remote, snow-clad woods of Tahoe National Forest. Behind the wheel, Michael was listening to music on his MP3 player while, in the passenger seat, his wife, Serena, was e-mailing on her tablet. In the back, the boys were all earphoned up. Peter, 12, was surfing on his smartphone; Adam, 11, was playing on his handheld gaming device; and Joey, 9, was watching a movie on the SUV's drop-down screen.

The only one not plugged in was Holly, the family's golden retriever, who was snoozing in the far back. She was a big, wide-bodied dog with boundless energy and the playfulness of a puppy. As smart as she was, she never fully grasped the concept that she wasn't a little lapdog. If a kid was sitting on the floor watching TV, Holly would pin him down by laying her 70-pound body across his legs. If she was in need of some scratching behind the ears, she'd lean against the closest family member and give a little moan. The family knew not to leave any food unattended on the coffee table. It wasn't that she would eat it (unless it was cheese); it was that her strong, wagging tail would sweep the food right onto the floor.

Holly loved playing with the kids, especially if there was a ball involved. During touch football games, she sometimes couldn't help herself and tackled the ball carrier. At the baseball field, she had run off with foul balls too many times to count (although she did bring them back).

Everyone considered Holly the friendliest dog in the neighborhood — everyone, that is, except the squirrels. She *hated* them. She would drop whatever she was doing — retrieving the morning paper, playing fetch, gnawing on a bone — to go after squirrels. She chased them up trees, rain gutters, bushes, and walls. No one knew what she would do if she ever caught one, because she never did.

Holly was lucky to be with the family on the trip to Tahoe, considering the trouble she had caused on their last Christmas vacation.

The Gerards had rented a three-bedroom house with a pool in a quiet neighborhood in the desert tourist town of Palm Springs, California. The house was only a block away from Serena's parents, who were throwing a big holiday reunion for their four married children and ten grandchildren. Because there wasn't room for everyone, the Gerards had opted to rent the nearby house. The owner agreed to let them bring Holly on the condition that she stay in the backyard or the screened-in porch and not inside. And that was only after Michael, an attorney who handled million-dollar negotiations, convinced him that the family's two-year-old retriever was well behaved, which she was — most of the time.

The first two days in Palm Springs, Holly enjoyed all the attention she was receiving from the Gerard kids' cousins. She splashed around in the pool with them for hours.

On the third night, Michael noticed that his kids and many of his nieces and nephews were spending way too much time on their handheld electronic devices. "You see each other a couple of times a year," he told them, "so why don't you put away your electronics and enjoy more face time with each other? I have an idea. Since it's Christmastime, go caroling."

To his surprise, the kids thought it was a decent idea, so off they went. Holly tagged along.

The next morning, Michael was walking the dog when a gray-haired man in a Hawaiian shirt, yellow Bermuda shorts, and long white socks and sandals stopped him and asked, "You're renting Mr. Clausen's house, right?"

"Yes, sir," replied Michael, noticing the man had a slight scowl.

"So those were your kids singing in the street last night? Because no children live on this block."

"My kids and their cousins were caroling through the neighborhood. I hope you enjoyed it."

"Well, I'm not making any accusations, but Rudolph is missing." He pointed to a miniature ceramic Christmas display of Santa and his reindeer. Rudolph the Red-Nosed Reindeer was not among them. "Could you kindly ask them if they might know where it is?" he said with a hint of sarcasm. "Maybe one of them took it as a prank."

Annoyed but remaining polite, Michael replied, "My kids wouldn't do that, but I will ask." Seeing Holly sniffing at the remaining 18-inch-high reindeers, he said, "Come, on, girl. Let's go home."

When Michael questioned his children and their cousins, they all swore they hadn't taken Rudolph, and he believed them.

The next morning Michael was walking Holly when he spotted the same neighbor. The man had his hands on his hips and was staring at his Christmas display. He turned and glared at Michael. The man spread his arms and said, "Now Donner and Blitzen are gone!"

Michael went over to him and said, "Sir, I talked to the kids. They didn't take your reindeer, nor do they know who did. Last night they were with me and the entire family."

"Well," growled the man, "I intend to catch the thief or thieves . . . and I know just how to do it."

The kids were getting ready to go over to their grandparents' the next morning when the doorbell rang. Peter answered the door and gulped when he saw who was there. He shouted toward the kitchen, "Uh, Dad? There's a policeman at the door. He wants to talk to you."

Perplexed, Michael hurried to the front door and said, "May I help you?"

"Do you have a golden retriever?" the officer asked.

"Yes, I do," said Michael. "What's this all about, sir?"

"If you don't mind, would you please come with me? And bring your dog."

With Holly by his side, Michael followed the officer to the house where the scowling man lived. As they walked up to the front door, Michael noticed that two more reindeer were missing.

The man stepped out, pointed toward Holly, and told the officer, "That's the thief!"

"What are you talking about?" Michael asked.

"I have unmistakable proof that your dog is a thieving, conniving canine! Come inside and I'll prove it."

They all went into the living room. "After Rudolph, Donner, and Blitzen disappeared, I set up a security camera last night," the man said. He turned on the TV. "Here's the video that it took." The camera clearly showed that during the night Holly had entered the front yard, sniffed around the Christmas display, and then snatched a reindeer — later identified as Dancer — in her mouth and trotted off.

"Aha!" declared the man. "See? It's your dog! Caught in the act!"

"But I don't understand," said Michael. "We keep her in the screened porch at night."

"Oh, really? Wait. There's more."

He fast-forwarded the video. "About ten minutes later, look what that mutt of yours did!" The video didn't lie: Holly returned and took off with another reindeer — later identified as Prancer.

"Do you deny that the thief is your dog?" the man said.

"No, it's definitely her."

"Where are my reindeer?" the man demanded.

"I don't know," Michael replied. "But I know how we might find them. There's one catch, though. I need to borrow one of your remaining reindeer."

After coaxing by the officer, the man agreed. Michael picked up Vixen and held it in front of Holly's nose. "Here, girl, take it." She eagerly gripped it in her mouth. "Okay, girl, go home. Go on."

Holly turned and strutted back toward the rental house as Michael, the neighbor, and the officer followed her. She ambled to a partially fenced area in the backyard that hid two garbage cans, where she dropped Vixen — right next to the missing Rudolph, Donner, Blitzen, Dancer, and Prancer. All were safe and undamaged.

The mystery of how she got out at night was quickly solved. An inspection of the enclosed back porch revealed that a screened panel was not secured to its frame, which no one had noticed until then. Holly had noticed. At night, she simply walked through the screen as if it was a drape, and roamed the neighborhood. Why she stole the reindeer, no one knew.

So it was understandable why Michael balked before caving in to the pleas of his wife and sons to take Holly on the family's Christmas vacation to Tahoe. "We're going to be in a vacation cabin out in the boonies," Serena had told him. "How much trouble could she cause?"

On the final hour of the long drive to the cabin, when the SUV began heading up the mountains, Michael suggested, "Hey, kids, turn off your electronics and take in the scenery."

"Hey, look!" shouted Joey. "Snow!"

"The pine trees look like they've been dusted in powdered sugar," said Serena.

"You'll be seeing tons more snow the higher we go," said Michael. "There was a big snowfall two days ago."

By the time they reached an elevation of 5,500 feet, more than a foot of snow covered the ground. Fortunately, the highway was plowed, but the lane that led to their remote rental cabin wasn't. The SUV, its tires sometimes spinning and whining, had a tough time reaching the house through the heavy snow.

After she jumped out of the vehicle into the snow, Holly leaped almost dolphin-like from one spot to another until her face was caked in the white stuff. She was having so much fun with her first snow experience that she accidentally plowed into Michael, who was carrying a cooler, and sent him sprawling.

Adam was the first to fling a snowball, and it smacked his little brother in the back of the head. Furious, Joey returned fire, missing Adam but hitting Peter in the shoulder. In retaliation, Peter stuffed a handful of snow down Joey's back.

Joining in the fun, Michael wrapped his burly arms around Peter and told Joey, "Here's your chance to get even." Joey scooped up a handful of snow and shoved it down Peter's back. While Michael was pinning his eldest son, Serena sneaked up on her husband and dumped a pile of snow on his head. Wanting in on the action, Holly jumped on Serena, knocking her to the ground.

Inside the lavish log cabin, the Gerards oohed and aahed. The top floor featured a master bedroom with its own deck and hot tub. The main floor had a spacious kitchen and a large family room dominated by a two-story-tall rock fireplace. Each bedroom had its own flat-screen TV. The house had every convenience a tech-happy family could want: cable TV, Blu-ray, gaming console, Wi-Fi, and high-speed Internet.

Shortly after they had settled in, Michael announced, "Let's put the electronics away and have some real fun!"

He had arranged for the owner to equip the cabin with inner tubes, snowshoes, and a map to a secret sledding slope about a half mile away. It was a picture-perfect winter day — sunny and in the 30s with only a hint of a breeze. Wearing snowshoes and dragging inner tubes, they headed for the hill. Holly tailed them, occasionally barking at a squirrel that was scurrying from one branch to another.

When the Gerards reached the slope, they discovered that it wasn't that secret, because there were at least a dozen other kids and grown-ups skimming down the hill on inner tubes, sleds, and toboggans. Adam, Peter, and Joey soon raced each other down the slope with Holly in hot pursuit, but the boys were too fast for her.

While the Gerards were working their way up after their third run, Holly went over to a rosy-cheeked toddler who was sliding on an inner tube on a much smaller slope. The boy was laughing as Holly ran next to him. Suddenly, she launched herself and, with perfect timing, landed right on his inner tube. It would have been funny except for two unintended consequences. She knocked the little boy off, and she punctured the inner tube with her nails, bringing an abrupt end to the ride.

Holly lumbered back toward the little boy, who was shrieking from fright and being comforted by his parents. The father stood up and angrily shooed the dog away. When Michael arrived, the man chewed him out, claiming that the "horrible dog" ruined the fun for his son. The mother was sitting in the snow, rocking the whimpering boy. "How could you let such an unruly dog loose? Why couldn't you keep her on a leash?"

Michael apologized repeatedly and pointed out that Holly loved people, especially kids, and was just playing. "I'll take my dog back to the cabin so she won't bother anyone," said Michael. "While I'm gone, please use my inner tube, and here's money for the one she ruined."

Judging by the position of her downward-pointing tail, Michael figured she knew she had done something wrong. She whined upon leaving the hill where everyone — except maybe the little boy — was having such a grand time.

"Holly, you're going to give me gray hair with your antics," said Michael.

As they neared the cabin, Michael noticed that a tall birch tree was bent from the weight of the snow and leaned perilously over the power and phone lines that

Christmas Surprise!

This coupon is worth one free homework pass!

It cannot be used on a test and has to be approved before use. Can be used for any subject that is taught by Mrs.Sanek.

went to the house. In fact, a wire had been fastened about halfway up the trunk and was attached to the deck railing in an effort to keep the tree from falling.

Inside, he told Holly, "Sorry, girl, but you have to stay here the rest of the day." When he left, he heard her sad barks.

During the night more snow fell, and the wind had picked up, creating some impressive drifts. The next morning, which was Christmas Eve, the boys began jumping off the deck into a four-foot snowbank. That looked like fun to Holly. She climbed onto a deck chair and table before leaping over the railing and disappearing into a drift, where the boys helped dig her out.

After a hike in the woods, the family made two forts and had a snowball fight. Holly got pelted the most, because she kept trying to bite the flying snowballs.

Later in the day, while Michael and the boys were building a huge snowman, Holly walked up the steps to the main deck and peered through the sliding glass door at Serena, who was preparing Christmas Eve dinner.

Suddenly, Holly spotted two squirrels that had the audacity to jump onto a bird feeder attached to a shepherd's hook on the deck. The dog went ballistic. Once she gained traction on the slushy deck, she charged after the furry intruders.

Seeing Holly bearing down on them, the pair did their best imitation of Rocky the Flying Squirrel and sailed off the bird feeder. Holly bounded up onto a large, round wrought-iron table only to watch them flee. She tried to stop, but because it was icy, she lost her footing and slid across the table and crashed into a seven-foot-tall portable outdoor gas heater. The impact caused the heater to topple over. As it fell, it clipped the wire that was restraining the snow-laden bent birch tree. When the wire broke, the tree dropped right onto the power, cable, and phone lines and brought them down.

The panicked dog scrambled off the deck and ran into the woods. Michael and the boys had watched the incredible chain of events unfold. Before anyone could react, Serena stepped out onto the deck and shouted, "The power is out!"

They began yelling at once, trying to explain to her what had happened. Because they were talking over each other, Serena was picking up only a few words, such as *squirrels*, *heater*, *wire*, *tree*, and *power lines*. Then the boys pointed at Holly, who had cautiously emerged from the woods. She looked bewildered and scared.

They brought the dog into the cabin so she wouldn't go near the downed wires. When Serena heard how they lost power, she stared at Holly and said, "How can such a sweet dog cause so much trouble?"

Michael pulled out his cell phone, hoping to call the owner. "Darn it," he groused. "I can't pick up a signal."

"Well, dinner is going to be ruined. What more can go wrong?"

"I'll drive to the nearest house — it can't be more than a couple of miles away — and use their landline to get a power company crew out here," said Michael. He patted his pockets and then asked Serena, "Do you have my keys?"

She shook her head. "No, you had them last."

"Okay, let me borrow yours and I'll look for mine later."

Serena bit her lip and said, "Sorry, Michael. In the rush to leave yesterday, I left them at home."

He thought for a moment and said, "I don't recall ever setting my keys down when we arrived. I had them in my hand when I was unloading . . ." Then he muttered, "Holly!"

"She's right here," said Serena. "What did she do?"

"Now I remember. Holly knocked me down when we first got here. I bet that's when I lost my keys. They're probably somewhere out there in the snow. We need to find them."

"That could take hours," she said.

"Well, then, I'll hike to the nearest house."

"It'll be dark before you get there. I think we should make do with what we have and deal with this tomorrow," Serena said.

"You realize that without power, we have no light, no heat — and we have no water, because the well pump needs electricity," Michael said.

Joey's face scrunched up as he asked, "Are we going to freeze to death?"

"Are we going to starve to death?" asked Adam, half in jest.

"I can see the headlines now: 'Family Dies in Wilderness,'" Peter joked.

"Listen, everyone," said Serena. "We can sit here and complain, 'Oh, woe is me,' or we can turn this into an adventure, a challenge."

Michael brightened up. "Serena, you're right! Let's make this a modern-day pioneer Christmas!"

"Michael," she said, "there's a barbecue grill outside and a bag of charcoal in the lower level. Get that fired up so I can finish cooking dinner.

"Joey, there are some candles and matches in the pantry. Flashlights, too. Bring them here. Peter and Adam, start bringing up the firewood that's stacked out back. We'll build a big fire in the fireplace for warmth. When you're done with that chore, fill pots with snow. We'll melt it for drinking water and flushing the toilets."

So on Christmas Eve, the Gerards enjoyed a delightful candlelight dinner of barbecued chicken (instead of roasted), baked potatoes (instead of mashed), and grilled corn on the cob (instead of corn pudding). Later, they sat in front of a blazing fire and stuffed themselves with s'mores and sang Christmas carols.

On Christmas morning, they opened presents that they had brought from home. Michael fired up the grill and made scrambled eggs and bacon for breakfast.

After getting dressed, the family hunted for the car keys in the snow. The process was slow and painstaking. "This isn't exactly how I planned to spend Christmas Day," Michael said. But no one complained. Meanwhile, Holly kept poking her nose in the snow and digging in various places.

After an hour, Joey shouted, "Hey, everyone, look at Holly!" There, at the bottom of the snow hole she had made, were the keys.

Minutes later, Michael drove to the closest neighbor and phoned the power company and the owner of the rental cabin, alerting them to the problem. When he returned to the house, he told the family, "Power won't be restored until tomorrow. We can pack up and go home, go to a motel, or stay here another night."

"Stay here another night!" they all shouted.

That evening the Gerards sat around the fire and played Monopoly and card games. No one bothered with their tablets or gaming devices. Maybe it was because the batteries on their gadgets were running low and there was no way to charge them. Or maybe it was because the kids were having such a good time they didn't need their electronics to be entertained.

Holly, of course, had no clue about the role she had played in this delightful Christmas. She was totally content, lying in front of the fire listening to the laughter of her human family.

The next year, the Gerards stayed home for the holidays. On Christmas Eve, they turned off the lights and TV and put away all their electronics. They lit their living room with candles and sang carols and played board games — and they decided that, yes, this would be their family tradition every Christmas Eve.

THE NIGHT VISITORS

Callie Bedford winced when she overheard her mother crying. The ten-year-old girl crouched down in the hallway and pressed her ear against her parents' bedroom door. Her late-night trip to the bathroom would just have to wait. *Is Mama sick again? Is that why she's crying?* Callie trembled at the thought and then eavesdropped.

"But, Mason, you said that after all the drastic changes they made at the plant, things would get better. You said that the worst was over."

"I know, Olivia, I know. That's what the bigwigs told us after they laid off half the workers and cut the salaries of us engineers. But the scuttlebutt is that they're going to shut down the plant sometime in the next two months."

Between her muffled sobs, Olivia blurted, "So there's no hope of saving the house?"

"I'm afraid not, sugar. The bank won't give me the time of day. They're going ahead with the foreclosure."

Callie's stomach churned. She had heard enough over the past few months to know what that term meant: The bank was starting legal proceedings to kick the family out of the house because her parents had fallen too far behind in the mortgage payments.

"Mason, I just can't believe all this is happening to us right before the holidays. We're going to lose a house that's been in your family for — what — four generations?"

"Great-grandfather Cornelius would be turning over in his grave if he knew this place will soon belong to the bank."

"I feel terrible," Olivia said, futilely trying to stifle her sobs. "This wouldn't have happened if I hadn't gotten sick and we didn't have to mortgage the house to pay the medical bills."

"Don't ever talk that way, Olivia. Remember our wedding vows: 'In sickness and in health.' It's worth every penny knowing your cancer is in remission."

"What are we going to tell Callie?"

"Nothing for now," Mason replied. "Let's not ruin the holidays for her."

"But we've always been honest with her, even when things looked grim during my illness."

"If she asks, just downplay it," Mason suggested. "She's well aware that we're pinching pennies."

"It's going to be a very lean Christmas," Olivia lamented before bursting into tears again.

Just then they heard a crash below their second-floor bedroom window. "Someone is on the porch!" Mason declared. He jumped out of bed, ran to the closet, and grabbed a baseball bat. "You stay here while I investigate. I'll yell if I need you to call 911."

Callie got up off the floor outside their bedroom door and quietly scooted toward her room, but she didn't make it before he stepped into the hallway and spotted her. He hid the bat behind his back, because he didn't want to alarm her. "Callie? What are you doing up? It's nearly midnight."

"I, uh, heard something outside."

"So did we. Keep your mama company while I check it out."

Mason hustled downstairs, flipped on the porch lights, and cautiously stepped outside. He saw that two large potted plants had been knocked over, leaving chunks of dirt and shards from the shattered clay pots on the wooden porch floor.

Hearing metal clanging in the unattached garage, he tiptoed to the side door. Gripping his bat in his right hand, he opened the door with his left and flicked the light switch. "Freeze!" he yelled. His eyes darted in every direction in the garage as he looked for the intruder. He found no one. However, a shovel and a rake were lying on the floor next to a tipped-over bag of potting soil. Dozens of nuts and bolts from an open plastic container were strewn all over his workbench. Fortunately, nothing was taken. He closed and locked the window, which he had left open.

Callie had a difficult time falling back to sleep. *Foreclosure!* The thought that she might be uprooted from the only home she knew overshadowed any concerns about a possible break-in. Like her parents, she loved the grand 110-year-old southern Victorian, which sat on an acre lot of magnolias, oaks, azaleas, gardenias, and crape myrtles. The charming yellow house with the dark green shutters was one of the prettiest in their small Mississippi Gulf Coast town. Passed down from generation to generation, the house still had the original oak floors in the living and dining rooms, tiger-wood built-in bookshelves in the library, tongue-and-groove bead board in the kitchen, a claw-foot tub in the master bathroom, and five working fireplaces. Callie always felt a certain comfort in the old house, as if the spirits of all the ancestors who had lived there were looking after her.

Nothing was said at the breakfast table about the family's financial woes. But when Callie returned home from school, she asked her mother point-blank, "Are we getting thrown out of our house?"

Olivia, who was cleaning in the living room, pressed her lips together and dusted the hand-carved mahogany mantel, trying to figure out what to say. "Land sakes, don't even think such a thought! This is Christmastime, a happy time. Let's have no more talk about the house. Now, would you please take out the garbage?"

As the petite fourth grader carried two bags to the metal cans behind the garage, she heard Mrs. Maloney, the feisty elderly widow next door, giggling in baby talk. "Oh, you are the *cutest* things! Yes, you are!"

Curious, Callie walked over to the fence that separated the two yards. From the girl's vantage point, it looked like the 85-year-old woman was talking to herself. "Hi, Mrs. Maloney," said Callie.

"Hello, Callie. Come for a spell and meet my new friends."

Not seeing anyone else, Callie thought, *Is she starting to lose her mind?* The girl decided to play along with what she assumed were Mrs. Maloney's imaginary friends.

When Callie entered the woman's backyard, she saw for the first time that Mrs. Maloney did indeed have company — three small raccoons. They were eating out of a dog dish on the patio only a few feet away from where the woman was sitting on a chair, resting her chin on her cane.

"Callie, meet Billy, Ray, and Cyrus."

"You named them after Miley Cyrus's dad?"

"Oh, I just love him," Mrs. Maloney said. "'Achy Breaky Heart' is my all-time favorite." Pointing to the raccoons, she said, "Sure as cornbread goes with greens, they are bewitchin'. Showed up 'bout a week ago, lookin' hungry, so I fed 'em. They came back the next day and the day after. I adopted 'em . . . or maybe they adopted me."

"Should you be feeding wild animals?"

"They're God's creatures. And they're hungry. They must be orphaned, 'cause I ain't seen hide or hair of the mama."

"They are cute. Are you keeping them as pets?"

"Heavens, no. After Anastasia died, God bless that beautiful dog, I said no more pets, and I'm stickin' to my promise. But it won't hurt if I help these orphans for a little bit. I don't want 'em totally dependent on me, so I'm fixin' to spread dry dog food over the yard so they can learn to forage for themselves. It's a cruel world, and only the strong survive. But then, I don't need to tell you 'bout stayin' alive. Your mama is a survivor."

When Callie returned home, she told her parents about the widow's new friends.

"Mrs. Maloney is a sweet lady with a heart of gold," said Olivia. "But it's dangerous to feed raccoons, because they can carry rabies and other diseases."

"And destructive, too," said Mason. "I remember the time Grandpa tamed a bunch of wild raccoons and had them eating out of his hand. Then one day he found them in the house, tearing up the cushions on the couch. Oh, was he mad! He shooed them out, got his shotgun, and fired in the air. He didn't have the stomach to kill them. Every time they showed up after that, he blasted that gun, until they got the message and never came back again."

A few days later, Callie helped Mrs. Maloney decorate her artificial Christmas tree. After they finished stringing the lights and putting up round painted ornaments made of tin, the widow insisted they take a break and snack on a piece of her pecan pie in the kitchen.

While they were eating, they heard an ornament fall to the hardwood floor in the living room and roll around. But instead of coming to a stop, it sounded like it continued to move on its own.

Callie hurried into the living room. "Oh, gracious me!" she yelled. "There's a raccoon in here . . . and he's playing with an ornament!"

Mrs. Maloney got up and, leaning on her cane, hobbled into the room. When she saw the young raccoon batting the metal ornament, she clucked, "Well, I'll be dipped in molasses and rolled in cornflakes! Ain't that somethin'?"

"Mrs. Maloney, it's a raccoon! In your house! We need to get it out of here!"

"I can't tell if that's Billy or Ray. They look so much alike. It's definitely not Cyrus. He has a much wider mask."

"Mrs. Maloney!"

"Oh, all right." The raccoon started waddling over to the woman, who bent over to get a closer look at the animal. "Now I can tell. It's Billy!" Wagging her finger at the critter, she said, "Shame on you, Billy. You're not welcome in my house. You have to go." Turning to the girl, she said, "Be a dear and open the front door." After Callie did, the woman tapped her cane loudly on the floor and coaxed the critter outside.

Suddenly, they heard something breaking in the kitchen. When they entered the room, they saw that Callie's plate and glass of milk had shattered on the floor. Her half-eaten slice of pie was gone. From the open lower-cabinet door, a container of oatmeal had spilled, along with a box of pancake mix. Two sets of tiny white raccoon footprints led to the kitchen door, where Callie caught a glimpse of a striped bushy tail slipping out the doggy door.

"Well, if that don't knock my stockin's off!" Mrs. Maloney exclaimed.

"What a mess!" said Callie. "I'll get Daddy to nail the doggy door shut so they can't get in again. Maybe you should stop feeding Billy, Ray, and Cyrus."

"Oh, I couldn't stop now," said Mrs. Maloney. "That wouldn't be fair to Lisa, Marie, and Presley."

"What? Who are they?"

"New raccoons. I'm guessin' Billy, Ray, and Cyrus are spreadin' the word that I'm an easy touch."

Callie shook her head. "This place will be swarming with raccoons."

"The Bible says, 'Be thou diligent to know the state of thy flocks, and look well to thy herds.'"

"Please tell me you're not planning on raising raccoons!"

Later, back home, Callie was helping her mother fix dinner when Olivia told her, "Money is tight right now. Would you be upset if we don't put up a Christmas tree this year?"

"No problem, Mama," Callie said, hiding her disappointment. "I had fun decorating Mrs. Maloney's tree, so I don't need to do it again." Olivia kissed the girl on the forehead and said, "I'm so lucky to have a daughter like you. Someday we'll recover from this financial pickle and have the fanciest tree and the best Christmas you can ever dream about."

That night, Callie couldn't sleep. She had been picking up bits and pieces from hushed conversations in the house: "The plant closes in January" . . . "No engineering jobs" . . . "Seeing a lawyer about the foreclosure" . . . "No money to start my own firm."

Callie fretted about the family's immediate future. *Where will we live? Will we be homeless? Will I have to go to a new school? Will Daddy find a new job? What will happen to us?*

About 11 P.M., she heard thumping and scratching directly overhead and then little footsteps. She got up and followed the sounds. Then she hustled down the hall and knocked on her parents' door. "Daddy," she called out softly. "There's something in the attic. I think it's a raccoon."

Mason groaned and stepped out in his T-shirt and Skivvies. He went up the narrow stairs to the attic, opened the door, and stuck his head inside. While he was waving the flashlight back and forth, the beam caught a pair of beady eyes.

"It's a raccoon!" he called down to Callie and Olivia, who were standing at the bottom of the stairs. "Oh, criminy! There's another one . . . and another one!" He closed the door and shook his head. "Can things get any worse?"

When he came down the steps, Olivia asked him, "What are you going to do?"

"Nothing," he replied. "Why bother? Let it be the bank's problem."

"Mason, we can't have raccoons living up there," Olivia said.

He sighed. "You're right. I'll see what I can do in the morning."

After breakfast, he brought out a ladder, climbed onto the gabled roof, and looked for holes. He didn't find any. However, when he examined the soffits — the undersides of the roof overhangs — he discovered that one of the vents had been yanked off. Convinced that was where the raccoons entered at night, he sealed it with a piece of metal. "Problem solved!" he declared.

That evening, Callie decided to write a poem to each of her parents as their Christmas gifts, hoping her words would cheer them up and show them how much she loved them. She planned to put the poems in separate boxes wrapped in paper she colored herself. Composing the first poem while on her bed, Callie heard loud thumping noises once again coming from the attic. "Daddy!" she shouted. "I think you trapped the raccoons *in* the attic instead of keeping them out!"

Another nighttime trip to the attic proved she was right.

The next morning, Mason came down for breakfast and asked Olivia, "Do we still have our old portable CD player?"

"Yes, in the hall closet."

"Good. Go through your CDs and pick out the most obnoxious heavy metal band you can find — the ones I can't stand. We're going to make it so uncomfortable for those raccoons that they'll flee and never return."

After breakfast, Mason opened up the soffit vent he had sealed. Then he and Callie went into the attic and set up a bright spotlight and CD player. "What CD did your mother choose?" he asked.

"Metallica."

"Good choice. The raccoons should hate them as much as I do."

He turned on the CD player full blast as songs such as "The Unforgiven" and "Nothing Else Matters" reverberated throughout the attic. Apparently, nothing else mattered to the critters except to get away from the bright light and loud, screeching music. The trio moved — but not out of the house. Instead they retreated to the most secluded corner of the attic, tucked between low, intersecting roofing beams.

Mason then played CDs of Megadeth, Black Sabbath, and Iron Maiden. But when he checked on the raccoons at lunchtime, they were still there.

"I give up," he sighed. "They win."

"Can we try one more thing?" Callie asked. "Let me spread mothballs and ammonia up there, because I read that raccoons hate those smells. I'm small, so I can get close to those tight corners."

"But the fumes can be dangerous."

"I can hold my breath for a long time."

Mason agreed, but only after he outfitted her with gloves, knee pads, and a scuba mask. While Olivia hovered by the attic door, Mason waited outside on the ladder, ready to seal off the soffit vent once he saw the raccoons leave.

Crawling on her hands and knees, Callie placed mothballs in the various corners and sprayed ammonia. Each time she neared the raccoons, they squeezed into another cramped section of the attic, until finally they departed through the open vent.

As she started to back out, Callie spotted a dust-covered two-foot-long narrow wooden box that was resting between wood beams. The box, which was completely hidden from view beyond two feet away, had a brass latch that was padlocked.

She had to drag it to the attic entrance, because it was so heavy. Callie and her mother then brought it into the kitchen, where Mason pried off the lock with a hammer and a screwdriver. When he opened it up, he let out a whistle of amazement. "Wow, will you look at this!"

The box was crammed with old coins, hundreds of them, mostly U.S. silver dollars and half-dollars, Indian ten-dollar gold pieces, and Liberty twenty-dollar gold pieces dating back to the 1800s.

Mason's hands began to shake. "These coins could be worth thousands of dollars!"

"Oh, Mason, wouldn't that be wonderful!" Olivia exclaimed. "Maybe this Christmas won't be so bad after all."

"I think our luck is finally turning around," he said.

"Where did the coins come from?" Callie asked.

"I don't know," Mason replied. "I suspect they belonged to your great-great-grandfather Cornelius."

"Wasn't he in the steel business in Birmingham and made lots of money?" Callie asked.

"That's right," her father said. "He was a little man — not more than five feet tall — but he was a big man in the industry. Family lore says he was also a miser. I think he hid these coins and went to his grave without ever telling anyone about them."

Two days later, Mason bounded into the house and bellowed, "Amazing news! I had an expert determine the value of the coins. And guess how much they're worth!"

"Don't keep us in suspense, Mason," Olivia begged. "Tell us!"

"Over . . . two . . . hundred . . . thousand . . . dollars!"

Olivia threw her hands into the air and shouted, "Praise the lord, we can save the house!"

"And there'll be enough left over to start my own engineering firm!"

"Thank you, raccoons!" shouted Callie.

Mason picked up Callie by the waist and twirled her around. Then he hugged Olivia. "Gals, get your jackets."

"Where are we going?" Olivia asked.

"To buy a Christmas tree!" he said. "The biggest and best one we can find!"

THE HOLIDAY HERO

Christmas Day, 1995

*Dear Diary: I got the best gift ever! A potbellied pig!!!
Well, actually I don't have it yet, but it's my Christmas
present!! How awesome is that??? I had opened all my presents
and got a pink wool sweater, a cool slap bracelet, some acid-
wash jeans, and cassettes of Madonna, Mariah Carey, and
Boyz II Men, and a poster of the* Friends *cast, and Aunt
Sophie stitched DANIELLE on a pillow for me.*

*I was cleaning up the wrapping paper when Mom
handed me another wrapped box. It was light as a feather.
When I opened it, there was a picture of the cutest brown-
and-white potbelly I have ever seen. My heart started beating
faster and I asked Mom, "Does this mean what I think it
means?" She nodded and said, "Yes, you're finally getting the*

pig you always wanted." I let out a squeal that would make any pig proud. I hugged Mom and she had tears in her eyes.

Then I hugged Daddy and I could tell he wasn't too thrilled, but he put on a happy face for me. As you know, Diary, Daddy has been against having any pets for like forever. But Mom and I have been working on him for months and months . . . and now I'm getting a pig!!! Daddy says the only reason he agreed is because I'm such a great kid and an honors student. Obviously!!! He also says when we get the pig, it's on a trial basis only. Yeah, right. Once Daddy sees how cute our new potbelly is, he'll fall in love.

December 26

Dear Diary: I'm so excited I can't stand it! Tomorrow we pick up my pig from the breeder's. Yippee!!! He's ten weeks old, weighs about eight pounds, and is ready to be loved, loved, loved!

I've almost got a name picked out. I've narrowed it down to four — Babe because I absolutely love the movie, Wilbur because Charlotte's Web is one of my favorite children's books, Porkchop because I think it's a cute name, and Hamlet because I'm trying to read Shakespeare (not easy!). I'll make up my mind once I hold my potbelly. I can't wait!

I've been reading everything I can find on the care, feeding, and training of potbellies. They are smart. They are *easily housebroken. They are clean. They don't have dander or smell bad. Pigs are the fourth-most intelligent animal behind humans, monkeys, and dolphins. (And they are way ahead in intelligence over jerks like Bryan Miller.)*

December 27
Dear Diary: I got him!!! I got my very own potbelly!!! Yaaaaaayyyy! I've decided to name him Hamlet. He's beyond cute.

Mom, Daddy, and I drove to the breeder's, which is an hour away from here. The farm had a bunch of the most adorable little pigs I had ever seen, but when I saw Hamlet, he was by far the cutest. I couldn't help it: I began to cry, I was so happy. Daddy insisted that we put Hamlet in a pet carrier, which we did, but that was a mistake.

On the way home, I was sitting in the backseat with the carrier on my lap, and Hamlet wasn't happy at all. His little nose kept pressing against the bars of the carrier door. I couldn't stand it any longer, so I opened the door and pulled him out. Wouldn't you know that at that same moment, Daddy swerved to avoid hitting a dog that was running across the road.

Hamlet fell out of my hands and onto the floor. He began squealing like he was being stabbed to death. The whole state of Virginia must have heard him. That wasn't the worst part, Diary. Oh, no. Pigs have a gland like a skunk, and when they get really, really scared, they let loose with a smell that's a hundred times worse than a rotten egg. Pee-yooo!!!

Daddy was steaming mad and wanted to turn around right then and there and give back the pig. I burst into tears and carried on. Thank goodness Mom calmed him down. We rolled down the windows even though it was cold outside. It was the only way to get rid of the icky smell. I picked up Hamlet and put him on a blanket on my lap, and he settled down and soon fell asleep. I love him.

December 28

Dear Diary: Hamlet slept through the night in the laundry room, which is now his own little area with his own little bed. We even have a litter box for him. He hasn't used it yet, but he will. He's smart. I fed him this morning, and he ate right out of my hand! He is the sweetest thing! Mom thinks so, too. We love the way he wiggles his tiny ears and twitches his nose. It's fun watching him explore the house. It wasn't so fun when I had to clean up his poop. It's a good thing Daddy was at work and didn't see it.

January 6, 1996

Dear Diary: Hamlet is soooo smart! Today I taught him to sit and now I'm teaching him to give kisses. As soon as I pick up the harness, he knows we're going for a walk, and he sort of does a little dance, because he loves walks. The neighbors stop and stare, and some of them come over and say how cute he is. I think he loves the attention.

He still doesn't want to use the litter box, and I'm tired of picking up his poop. Daddy got furious when he stepped in one of Hamlet's messes this morning — in his bare feet! Yuck! Daddy says if Hamlet isn't housebroken in the next week, "that pig is either gone or bacon." Daddy can say some mean things when he's angry.

Hamlet usually goes to the bathroom outside in one section of the yard, so I think I have to learn when he needs to go so we won't have a problem inside.

January 20
Dear Diary: Hamlet hasn't had any accidents in a week. Yaay! He does his business outside. He knows that when we leave, he has to stay in the laundry room, but otherwise he can roam in the house.

Hamlet loves to be cuddled, and it's so cute to see him come up to me and honk to be picked up. When I put him in my lap, he snuggles and falls asleep. He's so adorable!

February 17
Dear Diary: I went with Mom to Henderson's Market, and the produce manager knew about Hamlet, so he gave us

a big box of fruits and veggies that are still good but not good enough to sell in the store.

When we got home, I found two halves of overripe, juicy cantaloupe. I put half the melon in Hamlet's bowl, thinking he'd eat it there. But nooooo! He grabbed the cantaloupe with his teeth, and it flipped over his snout and covered his eyes. Mom and I split a gut laughing. But then Hamlet went into the dining room with cantaloupe juice dripping all over the carpeting! Oh, no! Oh, yes!

Mom yelled at him to stop. She never yells at him, so he got all freaked out and took off with the melon still covering his eyes. We ran after him and chased him through the dining room and living room and down the hallway and back into the kitchen before we could catch him. Oh, did he squeal! I took the melon away from him, escorted him outside, and then gave it back to him. I'll never feed him cantaloupe in the kitchen again.

Mom and I tried to clean up the cantaloupe juice on the carpet before Daddy got home from work, but he caught us. He was howling mad when he found out what had happened. (Momma can never tell a lie.)

May 5
Dear Diary: Just when I think Daddy is getting used to Hamlet (it's been over four months), my sweet, adorable pig

gets himself into a heap of trouble. I thought for sure that Daddy was going to get rid of him.

Here's what happened: Mom and I went out shopping and met up with Daddy for Sunday dinner at Minnelli's. When we came home, the family room was a DISASTER!!! The coffee table was overturned, the lamp was broken, Daddy's chair was torn, and stuffing was coming out of it. Hamlet was curled up in the corner with a piece of wrapping from Subway sticking out of his mouth.

I thought Daddy was going to have a heart attack!!! I don't know if I've ever seen him so angry. He was ranting and raving and scared poor Hamlet to death. Hamlet only made things worse by stinking up the place with that skunk smell he sends out when he's terrified. I put him outside and waited until Mom got Daddy to calm down, which took a long time.

And guess what, Diary. It was all Daddy's fault!!!

After Mom and I had left to go shopping, Daddy was home watching baseball in his easy chair. He was eating a Subway sandwich when he heard on the police scanner about a car wreck on Upton Road, so, being the good volunteer firefighter that he is, he ran out the door to help at the accident scene. He was in a real hurry and left the sandwich on his chair. When he put Hamlet in the laundry room, he forgot to latch the door.

While Daddy was gone, Hamlet opened the door and sniffed out the sandwich and jumped on Daddy's chair. Hamlet probably thought there was more food in the chair, because he dug into the crease between the seat and the back and tore it. He knocked over the table and lamp when he jumped off.

Daddy said Hamlet had to go, so naturally I burst into tears and begged and pleaded. Mom reminded Daddy that Hamlet has been a good pet and that none of this would have happened had Daddy put away his sandwich and latched the laundry room door. Hamlet was simply doing what pigs do — rooting for food.

Daddy admitted she was right, but he still wasn't happy about it. Thank goodness Mom is on my side or I'd lose Hamlet for sure.

July 21
Dear Diary: I had the super-best time at my pajama party last night . . . or should I say this morning?? Amber, Grace, Charlotte, Stacie, and Rhiannon stayed up until three. I was the last one to fall asleep. They kept calling me "the baby," because I'm the last in our group to turn 14.

Hamlet, as usual, hammed it up with the girls. They were adoring him the whole night, and was he enjoying all the attention! He wanted to sit in Grace's lap, but that was a problem, because he weighs 60 pounds now. He tried to stay up with us but he couldn't make it. He fell asleep on the floor in the family room with all four of his legs and his nose sticking straight up in the air. They thought that was hilarious, but that's the way he likes to sleep. And he snores! When he's out like that, he's hard to wake up. Stacie had the bright idea to balance a paper cup on his snout, and he didn't even stir! It was so funny we took a picture.

October 13

Dear Diary: I don't think Daddy will ever accept Hamlet. Once again, just when I think everything is okay between them, something bad happens. Ugh!

Today Daddy and Uncle Dave were watching the football game in the family room, and Hamlet was minding his own business when they started jumping up and down because the Redskins had scored a touchdown. Uncle Dave knocked over the bowl of chips, so naturally Hamlet ran over to help "vacuum" them up. Daddy didn't see him. When Daddy stepped back, he flipped over Hamlet and landed hard on his hand, trying to break his fall.

Daddy hurt his middle finger, and it started to swell and turn black and blue. He said he thought it was broken, so Mom took him to the hospital, and sure enough, Daddy came back with a splint on his finger.

He didn't say anything to me, but I knew what he was thinking. He wishes Hamlet was gone for good.

December 16
Dear Diary: This is the most EMBARRASSING day of my life!!!

This morning Hamlet got out through the backyard gate and walked the whole five blocks to school! I guess he missed me because I was gone the whole weekend at Aunt Lucille's, and I didn't get back until after he was sound asleep. Then I overslept this morning and rushed out without saying anything to him.

He climbed up the school steps and waited by the front entrance. Mr. Marks, the janitor, didn't know that, so when he opened the door from the inside, Hamlet walked right in! Mr. Marks started yelling at him and chased him down the hall. Naturally, Hamlet was scared, so he squealed real loud and set off another one of his stink bombs.

Teachers opened their classroom doors to see what the commotion was about. When they saw Hamlet, they started chasing him, too. I was in Miss Landowski's first-period honors English class. As soon as I heard the squealing, I knew it was Hamlet. Miss Landowski ordered everyone to remain at their desks. I ignored her and ran into the hall. I saw Mr.

Marks slip and fall. Mrs. Cameron, Mr. King, and a bunch of kids were running after poor Hamlet.

I yelled at the top of my lungs for everyone to stop! Hamlet was by the principal's office, and wouldn't you know, at that very moment, Mrs. Jorgensen stepped out and Hamlet ran right past her. She screamed and started jumping up and down.

I rushed right in and found Hamlet hiding behind Mrs. Jorgensen's desk. He was so glad to see me. I hugged him, but when he saw all the people who had crowded into the office, he panicked again and stunk up the place.

Everyone started talking all at once, and I had a hard time explaining that Hamlet was my pet, that he was a good pig, and that I had absolutely no idea how he ended up in school. The teachers and students started to laugh, but Mrs. Jorgensen didn't find it funny. She demanded to know if I had brought Hamlet to school as a joke.

I told her absolutely not and that Hamlet had never run away from home before.

Mrs. Landowski stuck up for me and reminded her that I've never been in trouble and that I'm a model student. Mrs. Jorgensen did that "harumph" thing she does when she admits she's wrong but won't say it. She made me call Mom, who was horrified when I told her what Hamlet did. Mom ran all the way to school and brought Hamlet's harness and took him home. I think she was as embarrassed as I was. No, that's not true. No one could be as embarrassed as I was.

I wish I could have gone home with Mom. When I returned to class, that jerk Bryan Miller said, "Your brother sure knows how to ham it up." Everyone laughed. I wanted to die. All day long I got teased. Sean Toomey said I was doing my "Christmas slopping," and kids started calling me "the Bride of Frankenswine."

I was HUMILIATED!! Someday I'll laugh about this, but not now.

December 17
Dear Diary: This is the worst day of my life!! No, it's the second worst. The worst day will be Saturday, because that's the day Hamlet will be taken away from me.

Daddy announced that we could no longer keep Hamlet, and that the school incident was the last straw. I cried and went down on my knees, begging him to let Hamlet stay. Daddy says his mind is made up, and there's nothing I or Mom can say or do that will change his mind. He can be so stubborn!

Daddy has found a farm for Hamlet. I have only three more days left with the greatest pet a girl could hope to have.

Christmas Surprise!

This coupon is worth one free homework pass!

It cannot be used on a test and has to be approved before use. Can be used for any subject that is taught by Mrs.Sanek.

This is going to be the most HORRIBLE Christmas ever! I don't know what I will do without Hamlet. He's my best friend and has taught me so much about love and companionship. No matter how sad or stressed I am, his happy honks and wiggly snout always make me laugh. Even if Daddy never liked him, Hamlet is part of this family. I'm going to miss his wagging tail and the silly things he does. The smudges on this page are from my tears. Sorry. I just can't stop crying.

December 22
Dear Diary: Mom, Daddy, and I nearly died Friday night!!! If it hadn't been for Hamlet, we'd all be DEAD!!! He saved our lives!!!

I'm still shaking. The gas furnace had been acting up lately, and Daddy said we probably needed to get it fixed. Then we had a two-hour power outage Friday morning from that snowstorm, and the furnace didn't want to kick on. But Daddy got it working again.

I had a headache and felt like throwing up when I went to bed that night. I thought it was because I was so stressed out, knowing that Hamlet would be gone in the morning. He was acting kind of weird and restless. It was almost like he knew he was being kicked out of the house for good.

Mom said she wasn't feeling well and thought she was coming down with the flu. Daddy complained of a bad headache and took some aspirin.

I was almost asleep when I heard Hamlet banging against the laundry room door over and over. He grunted and honked. Then he got really crazy and snorted and squealed. I heard Daddy yelling, so I got out of bed to see what the matter was, but I was so dizzy I fell to the floor. The next thing I remember is Daddy helping me up and shouting, "Get out of the house right now and get Hamlet out of here, too!" I threw on my coat and got my boots on and went outside in the snow with Hamlet. I was still dizzy and I didn't know what was happening. Daddy put a blanket around Mom and carried her out of the house. She looked like she had almost passed out. Daddy kept telling us to breathe deeply. Even though the air was cold, it felt good. I still wasn't sure what was going on until he said, "We have carbon monoxide poisoning!"

From science class, I know that carbon monoxide is a colorless, odorless, tasteless gas that can kill you.

Daddy called 911, and the ambulance came and took us to the hospital. Poor Hamlet had to stay behind in the toolshed next to the house. At the hospital, they took samples of our blood and found out that Daddy was right. We had a high level of carbon monoxide in our blood, so they gave us oxygen. The doctor said that if we had stayed in the house much longer, we'd all be dead! Thank goodness Hamlet was there to save our lives.

Daddy can't get rid of him now. He just can't!

December 23

Dear Diary: Daddy says Hamlet can stay!!! I'm soooo happy!!!

After what Hamlet did, Daddy says he's willing to put up with "that darn pig." (Those are Daddy's words.) I think Daddy is finally realizing what an awesome pet Hamlet really is.

We couldn't move back into our house until this afternoon, because the furnace had to be repaired and tested first. Daddy even installed a carbon monoxide detector.

December 25

Dear Diary: This was the best Christmas EVER!!! The only thing I ever wanted was to keep Hamlet. And now I have him for life!

I got some cool presents, mostly clothes. But the best gift was one that wasn't for me. Daddy gave Hamlet a beautiful leather collar with fake rubies and sapphires, because he said it was fit for a prince like Shakespeare's Hamlet. And you know what my sweet prince of a pig did? He gave Daddy one big kiss, smack on the lips!!!

CATMAN'S CHRISTMAS SURPRISE

Never before had Butch Jacobs been so excited about returning to school after the holiday break. As he drove into the parking lot, students and teachers stared at him — or rather at his car. By the time he rolled his bright orange 1969 Dodge Charger to a stop, a crowd had gathered around the vehicle.

"The General Lee!" someone shouted. "Cool!" declared another voice. "Are you Bo or Luke?" a girl asked.

Butch stepped out of the car and grinned, because he was driving the make and model of the General Lee, the car that had become famous in the hit television series *The Dukes of Hazzard*. The action-comedy show, which ran from 1979 to 1985, featured the adventures of two cousins, Bo and Luke Duke, who raced around in their souped-up Charger while outwitting corrupt county commissioner Boss Hogg.

"Yee-haw!" yelled a classmate. Then he belted out lines from the show's theme song.

Unlike the customized General Lee, Butch's vehicle was dented and rusty and had a temperamental transmission. But he didn't care, because it was his very own car. Not bad for a 16-year-old ranch kid.

"Where did you get such an awesome car?" a student asked.

"It's a Christmas present," Butch replied. "And I have my cat to thank for it."

Catman was not your typical barn cat. He was a spunky orange-yellow mix of who-knew-what that loved to perch on fence posts and rooftops and barn rafters as though he was lording over the ranch animals. Nothing was too high for him to climb, not even the old, rickety 40-foot-tall windmill that the Jacobs family kept as a reminder of their ancestors who had first worked the ranch a hundred years earlier.

From up high, the crazy cat would often launch himself into the air and, with his legs spread out and tail acting as a rudder, jump onto the backs of ranch hands and cows and horses. Needless to say, neither man nor beast was particularly pleased with the cat's high jinks.

Butch's 14-year-old sister, Amy, had originally named the cat Cornbread when he was a kitten. But it didn't stick. Because of his leaping abilities, the family began calling him Catman, a play on the name of the Caped Crusader, Batman.

Although he wasn't the biggest, Catman was the toughest of the six cats on the Jacobs' North Dakota cattle ranch. He was by far the best mouser, often attacking unsuspecting rodents from the air with one of his patented dive bombs.

If any fellow cat tried to question his authority, the challenger ended up licking his or her wounds. Catman didn't fear any animal, including the bulls. Despite his toughness, he enjoyed the company of humans and liked to be petted and scratched behind the ears and at the base of his tail. But he had no desire to live indoors, even in the winter. The ranch was his domain, and the barn was his castle.

Catman had a special friendship with Butch and often followed the young man on his daily chores on the Double J Ranch. The spread was named after John Jacobs, the pioneer who staked out the land in the 1880s. The first son in every succeeding generation was a John, although each went by a nickname rather than have a Roman numeral after his name. That was why John Jacobs V was called Butch.

His father, Rusty — he with the buzz-cut red hair — was a no-nonsense man who believed that hard work was good for the soul and that everyone must pull his fair share on the ranch, no matter how young or old. Whatever job had to get done, you had better give it your all. To Rusty, "good enough" was not good enough. His word was his bond, and he expected the same of his family and ranch hands. If you said you were going to do something, you'd better darn well do it.

Butch admired and respected his dad and shared his strong work ethic. That was why on a blustery February afternoon in 1986, the young lad didn't complain when he came home from school to an empty house and found a note telling him to split a rick of wood; never mind that he had loads of homework. His mother, Martha, and sister, Amy, wouldn't be back until 6 P.M., and Rusty was working at a distant location with the ranch hands.

After fortifying himself with a cup of hot chocolate, Butch walked out to the woodshed, where he picked up a six-pound splitting maul — an iron wedge with a handle that looks like an ax — and headed to a pile of foot-long logs. He placed a log on its end on the chopping block, raised the maul over his head, and with one downward swing split the wood neatly in two. He repeated the process a few dozen times. Despite temperatures in the upper 20s, he worked up a sweat. Nearby, on the roof of the woodshed, Catman watched him with interest, purring and prancing in circles.

When it was time for Butch to load the split logs into the wood box, Catman leaped from the roof onto the young man's broad shoulders. "Hey, you crazy cat," said Butch. "What do you want?"

Catman leaned over and purred loudly in Butch's ear and remained perched on his shoulder like a parrot. Even when Butch bent down to load his arms with wood, the cat didn't budge. "Catman, you weigh too much to be on my back. Get off." Butch reached around, picked up the cat, and lowered him to the ground. Catman didn't stay there long. As soon as Butch bent over to pick up another bundle of wood, the cat jumped onto his shoulders again and leaned against his head. "Catman, you're beginning to be a pain in the neck — and I mean that in every way possible," said Butch, half amused and half annoyed.

Butch had just finished loading the wood box when he heard a distinctive moo in the distance. Having lived all his life on the ranch, he had a good idea of what the sound meant: A cow was in trouble.

With his feline friend bounding in the ankle-deep snow behind him, Butch trekked toward a clump of barren trees several hundred yards away. When he reached the other side, he saw that a black heifer had slipped off a snowy embankment and fallen into an icy shallow pond. "She's in trouble and she's panicking," he said to Catman. Butch dashed to the barn, where he grabbed a lasso, and sprinted back to the pond.

On his third try, he lassoed the terrified heifer around the neck, and as his muscles burned from exertion, he slowly dragged her out. When she was safe, the exhausted lad lay in the snow to rest. From somewhere, Catman jumped right onto his stomach, causing Butch to double up and groan.

At the dinner table that night, Rusty said, "I'm proud of you, son. You saved the life of a cow in distress."

"Thanks, Dad." Hearing praise from his father meant a lot to Butch, because Rusty was a little stingy when it came to giving out compliments.

After dinner Rusty decided the cow could use some straw bedding instead of lying on the cold, snowy ground. Wearing lighted miner's hats, Rusty and Butch each carried a bale of straw down toward the pond, near where the cow was resting. Although the bales weren't too heavy, they were awkward to carry that far — especially when Catman was clinging to the top of the one Butch was lugging. After father and son spread out the straw, Rusty led the cow to the new straw bed.

On the way back to the house, Butch figured that since his dad was in such a good mood, it was the perfect time to bring up a subject near and dear to the lad's heart. "Um, Dad, I was thinking . . ."

"That's always a bad sign," Rusty interjected, flashing his dry sense of humor.

"Now that I'm sixteen and have my driver's license, what do you think about me getting a car?"

"Why do you need a car? We can fix up the green pickup. You've been driving it on the ranch since you were thirteen."

"Dad, that's a 1960 Ford that's so rusted out you can see the ground through the floorboards. It's not fit to drive on the road. I was thinking of a car for school and to run errands for you and Mom."

"Oh? And do you have a particular car in mind?"

"Uncle Jim has a friend who owns a 1969 Dodge Charger that has one hundred and twenty thousand miles on it. He says it's in decent shape and he'll sell it to me for twenty-two hundred dollars. From the birthday money I've saved up, I have over a thousand dollars. Do you think that maybe you and Mom could cover the rest?"

"Sure," replied Rusty, and he quickly added, "when a cat can fly."

Butch hated that expression. It was his father's way of saying "There's no chance." When Martha had suggested that she and Rusty join a book club in town, he replied, "Sure, when a cat can fly." When Amy asked him if she could dye her hair pink, he replied, "Sure, when a cat can fly."

"But, Dad, I'm serious about the car," said Butch.

"So am I, son. And I'm a man of my word."

Not much more was said about buying a car, and life on the ranch continued to hum along on its seasonal rhythms. Before and after school during calving time, Butch helped with feeding, tagging, vaccinating, and weaning the calves and moving the cattle from pasture to pasture. He tended to the horses and fixed fences, repaired engines and dug ditches, and maintained irrigation equipment.

Catman continued to "oversee" the ranch from various high vantage points, often leaping onto an unsuspecting bull, horse, or ranch hand. He still loved to jump onto Butch's shoulders, confident that the young man would not fling him off in annoyance as some of the ranch hands were known to do.

Whenever the chicken-house door was open, he liked to jump at the chickens, trying to scare them. But they mostly looked the other way, because they had figured out the scamp was just playing and didn't really want to hurt them. Besides, some of the bigger chickens had made it clear to him not to get too close to them.

When Catman felt really energetic, he tagged along with Ajax, the Border collie, who helped keep the cattle in line. In fact, there were times when the cat acted more like a dog, crouching low in the grass and springing up at a wayward calf to guide it back toward the herd.

One blustery December afternoon, Catman and Ajax set out across the pasture with Butch and Rusty, who wanted to check on a pregnant cow that had been sick. During the trek, Butch mentioned the old Dodge Charger again. "It's still for sale," Butch reminded his dad. "Do you think you could help me buy it? You know, as a Christmas present?"

"Sure," Rusty replied. "When a cat can fly."

As the pair and their two four-legged companions neared the pond, they spotted a flock of mallards resting in the shallow water next to the embankment. Catman, being Catman, sauntered to the top of the embankment, looked down on the ducks, and without any hesitation, dived after them.

With all four legs spread out, he hit dead center of the flock, triggering an explosion of alarmed quacking and wing flapping.

The ducks all took flight — except for one. It was furiously beating its wings, but getting nowhere fast because there was something different about it. Finally, like an overloaded cargo plane, it slowly got airborne and veered out over the pond about four feet above the water.

At first, Butch's brain couldn't quite process what his eyes were seeing. The same with Rusty. They stood in disbelief at the sight. There was Catman flying on the back of a duck!

Butch couldn't tell who was more scared — the yowling cat or the squawking duck. Catman had wrapped his forelegs around the duck's neck in a death grip as the terrified bird listed to the right under the weight of his unwanted passenger.

"Dad, is this really happening?" Butch asked.

"I see it, but I don't believe it," Rusty murmured.

The frantic duck kept flapping its wings in a desperate attempt to gain more altitude, while the terrified cat wanted down. Moments later, the bird turned around and made a low pass that skimmed the top of the embankment a few yards from where Butch, Rusty, and Ajax stood rooted in astonishment.

Ajax was the first of the three to snap out of their shock. He bounded after the low-flying, duck-clutching cat, jumped up, and knocked the mallard out of the air, causing Catman and the bird to crash.

The petrified cat rolled onto his feet, scrambled under a bush, and hid there. Meanwhile, the shaken mallard took off again — this time without its heavy load — and flew away in the evening sky.

When the world's first duck-flying feline finally emerged from the bush, he ran to Butch and jumped into his arms. While trying to calm the still-shaking cat, Butch turned to his dad and said, "No one is going to believe what we just saw."

"I'm a witness to it, and I still don't believe it," Rusty replied, shaking his head.

After finding the pregnant cow and determining that she seemed fine, Butch and his dad headed back to the ranch house with Catman and Ajax. About halfway there, Butch was struck with a particularly happy thought. He let out a whoop and shouted, "Thanks, Dad! You're the best!"

Startled, Rusty replied, "What are you talking about?"

"The car. You said you would pay the balance of the car for Christmas when a cat can fly. Well, we just saw Catman fly! And, like you always say, you're a man of your word. Whoo-hoo!"

And that's how Butch got his Dodge Charger for Christmas . . . and Amy got her pink hair . . . and Martha got her husband to join the monthly book club.

ABOUT THE AUTHOR

Allan Zullo is the author of more than 100 nonfiction books on subjects ranging from sports and the supernatural to history and animals.

He has written the bestselling Haunted Kids series, published by Scholastic, which is filled with chilling stories based on, or inspired by, documented cases from the files of ghost hunters. Allan also has introduced Scholastic readers to the Ten True Tales series, about people who have met the challenges of dangerous, sometimes life-threatening, situations. Among his animal-themed books, he has authored *The Dog Who Saved Christmas and Other True Animal Tales*; *Christmas Miracle Pets: Animals Who Saved the Day*; *Bad Pets: True Tales of Misbehaving Pets*; and *Bad Pets on the Loose*.

Allan, the father of two grown daughters and the grandfather of five, lives with his wife, Kathryn, on the side of a mountain near Asheville, North Carolina. To learn more about the author, visit his website at www.allanzullo.com.